ADD A PLACE AT YOUR TABLE

FORTY YEARS OF COOKING AND SHARING

TONI CAPORELLO

www.biologicalcuisine.com

PUBLISHED BY ANTONELLA CAPORELLO
FIRST EDITION

ISBN 978-1-105-96244-8

9 781105 962448

For all home cooks

PHOTOGRAPHS
SILVANO GAI
TONI CAPORELLO

FORMATTING
SILVANO GAI

EDITING
MARCO FERRARIS
ROSSANA ANTONIOLI

Welcome

"Perfection is achieved not when there is nothing more to add,
but when there is nothing left to take away."

Antoine de Saint-Exupery

"Add a Place at your Table" is an expression that reflects the renowned Italian hospitality and, since I grew up in Italy, it's an integral part of my cultural heritage.

We always welcome an unexpected guest, and we make room for him or her at our table because we know that, even though the portions become smaller, the fun becomes greater. My recipes are based on the Mediterranean diet not only because it has been proven over and over again to be healthy and nutritious but also because it "emphasizes values of hospitality, neighborliness, intercultural dialogue and creativity, and a way of life guided by respect for diversity" as UNESCO states as the reasons for including it in its Representative List of the Intangible Cultural Heritage of Humanity.

When it comes to cooking, I have adopted Antoine de Saint-Exupery's principle as my guiding rule. My food must be fresh, organic, wholesome, unprocessed, and seasonal to provide all the beneficial elements necessary for our well-being, maintain a healthy weight, and prevent illnesses.

I call it Biological Cuisine, and I have created a blog about it, hoping to convince more people to adopt it.

Biological Cuisine is what the adjective implies: Bio-Logical, i.e., in harmony with our body. In reality, I cannot claim to have invented anything new. I have given a logical name to a way of cooking that already existed when we had no other choice than to make our food from scratch with naturally wholesome ingredients.

It should be intuitive that the food that we introduce into our body ought to be compatible with our biology, which means made of the same elements that our organism can efficiently process and assimilate.

Unfortunately, this is not always the case nowadays, especially in industrialized countries and particularly in the United States.

Imagine your body as a barrel into which you pour all kinds of good and bad things. In some measure, the good ones compensate for the bad ones, but we all know that often the latter

Cartoon by Dan Reynold, reproduced with the author's permission (processed food, alcohol, smoking, emotional and physical stress, fatigue, lack of sleep, etc.) tend to outnumber the former. Sooner or later, the barrel overflows, and we become sick. Over time, our immune system has been weakened by our bad habits, and it is no longer able to maintain a positive balance.

Unfortunately, we often underestimate the importance of our digestive system and make up different excuses that range from the lack of time and budget limitations to prioritizing work or our children's sports practices over cooking. By doing so, we often end up eating the wrong kinds of food, which in today's fast-paced lifestyle is often the most readily available, i.e., processed food.

In the past seventy years, the food industry has grown dramatically. To remain competitive, extend the shelf life of products, maintain their freshness, and make food tasty and appealing, it has resorted to adding more chemicals, preservatives, salt, hydrogenated fats, and high-fructose corn syrup. Over time, the convenience of processed food has become inversely proportional to its quality. Consumers are given the deceiving impression of saving time and money by eating ready-made food instead of cooking it from scratch. In reality, they will spend that time and money trying to heal all the ailments caused by an artificial diet devoid of our bodies needs.

To our partial justification, I must say that most foods are no longer what they used to be. Fruits and vegetables no longer come from familiar locations such as local farms and markets but from extensive monocultures or from huge greenhouses that can only exist with intensive synthetic pesticides and fertilizers. In both cases, produce is forced to grow fast, picked well before it's mature, and then refrigerated and shipped to warehouses where gases take care of its ripening just before the produce is ready to be transferred where it is sold. What you've just read shouldn't surprise you if you have ever picked some fruit from a garden: that juicy, rosy peach that ripened in the orchard will not stay fresh more than a few days without spoiling, even if you put it in your refrigerator. This is because of the way Mother Nature created it: if it's not used after being separated from the tree, it is supposed to rot to return its nutrients to the soil.

Have you have wondered why instead, those peaches from the southern hemisphere make such a beautiful display in our American supermarkets in February and stay fresh for days, even after traveling thousands of miles? Or why those perfect apples never shrivel but instead decay from the inside out? If you haven't, I suggest that you start questioning what has been applied to them and what remains of their nutritional value.

Also, the butcher is rarely the familiar face with a white apron that used to travel to small, clean farms to choose the animals to butcher in the back of his shop.

Slaughterhouses have become huge industrial plants that process tons of meat per hour, from animals that have been raised in quarters so cramped and in such unhealthy conditions that they had to be pumped with antibiotics to survive until the time of their demise.

Remember when the baker used to be the guy down the street who stayed up all night to make the bread that smelled heavenly while it was baking? Nowadays, most bread is pre-baked in huge industrial bakeries and then shipped to supermarkets hundreds of miles away, where they finish cooking it and where we buy it. For this process to work, many chemicals must be added to the dough, making what used to be one of our staple foods a much less desirable nutritional component of our diet.

While we still cannot resist the enticement of that delicious white bread, our body is already rebelling against the genetically engineered, pesticide-laden, and bleached grains used to make it.

I remember when food intolerances were a rarity and diet choices were based on taste, personal preference, or religion, but very infrequently on allergies and intolerances. Today, you can no longer have a dinner party without asking your guests in advance what foods they need to avoid.

Our grandmothers – and in many cases also our mothers - didn't need to choose between organic and non-organic ingredients. The ingredients they bought were organic, period. They didn't have to bother reading packaged food labels as we do today, simply because packaged food didn't exist or was made with a few basic ingredients. They didn't need to educate themselves about the risks posed by all the chemicals added to foods either. They indeed had to spend more time shopping. After all, food spoiled faster, more time cooking because almost everything had to be made from scratch, and they didn't have the fantastic selection of food we have nowadays. They didn't have to worry about Type 2 diabetes, cardiovascular diseases, obesity, and an array of auto-immune and inflammatory conditions that seem to have sprouted out of nowhere in the last two decades and that - I suspect - are the consequence of our bad eating habits.

As my mother used to say, "You don't pay back your debt on the same day you make it. You pay later and with interest." All the bad things we introduce into our bodies add up over time, and we end up paying our dues when we least expect it and with interest. Or, if you prefer to use an American proverb, "There isn't such thing as a free lunch," and, even if an inexpensive meal (as in "fast-food inexpensive") might seem convenient, it comes with a hidden and costly price tag.

You don't need a gourmet kitchen, expensive pots, and pans, complicated food processors, or extensive training to become a good cook. People have cooked for generations in tiny and modestly equipped kitchens with marvelous results. Like most other skills, cooking improves over time, by trial and error.

When in doubt, keep it simple. Simplify your life and shorten your shopping list by using fewer spices and condiments.

As we all know, nobody is perfect, and I'm the first one who needs some indulgence. Once a week or on particular occasions, I need to cook and eat something richer and tastier. I can be very good all week if I know that I can reward myself with a particular dish that I'm craving.

Looking forward to it helps me avoid straying from my guidelines or plan to compensate for the extra calories (for example, by exercising a little more). The key to a bit of indulgence is to do it in moderation and not make it a habit.

While using this cookbook, please remember that mine are only guidelines. I'm not a certified dietician or a nutritionist, and my recommendations are based only on my own experience — a lifetime of it, but still just my personal opinion and advice.

If you decide to follow my culinary tenets, keep in mind that cooking is an act of love towards yourself and the people you love, it's worth every minute of your time and every penny of your hard-earned money, and, most of all, it's fun, rewarding, and sexy.

CONTENTS

Zucchini Galette   Page   19
Eggplant towers   Page   21
Frittata with zucchini   Page   23
Focaccia   Page   25
Tomato, Mozzarella and Egg   Page   27
Russian Salad   Page   28
Variety   Page   30
Pantesca salad   Page   37
Tuna and Cannellini Salad   Page   39
Carrot Salad   Page   41
Radicchio Orange and Fennel   Page   43
Celery Root Salad   Page   45
Belgian Endive and Fennel   Page   47
Chicken Salad   Page   49
Fennel, Beet and Goat Cheese   Page   51
With a grain of salt   Page   52
Fettuccine with basil pesto   Page   59
Orecchiette with broccoli rabe   Page   61
Zucchini Spaghetti   Page   63

Roman Gnocchi   Page 65
Polenta   Page 67
Pizza! Pizza!   Page 68
Pizza Margherita   Page 73
Asparagus Risotto   Page 77
Riso and Zucca   Page 79
Mushroom Risotto   Page 81
Rice and Green Peas   Page 83
Chickpea soup   Page 85
Squash soup   Page 87
White beans and rice soup   Page 89
The eye also wants its share   Page 90
Halibut 'en papillotte'   Page 97
Finnish Salmon Pasty   Page 99
Black cod with olives and capers Page 101
Salmon with orange and mint   Page 103
Halibut with basil pesto   Page 105
Salmon cakes   Page 107
Mediterranean salmon   Page 109
Of Mushrooms and Marmalade   Page 110
Chicken Cacciatore   Page 117
Veal with Tuna Sauce   Page 119
Rabbit with Olives   Page 121

Turkey tenderloin with prunes	Page 123
Chicken Tenders with Lemon	Page 125
Shortcuts	Page 126
Orange Ring Cake	Page 133
Holiday Cream	Page 135
Avocado Parfait	Page 137
Meringata	Page 139
Fruit Salad	Page 141
A Secret Recipe	Page 142
Apple Strudel	Page 144
Peach Tiramisù	Page 147
Poached Pears	Page 149
Apple Cream Torte	Page 151
Cornmeal cookies	Page 153
Cantucci	Page 155
Zaeti	Page 157
Hazelnut Amaretti	Page 159
Zabaione	Page 161
Hazelnut Cake	Page 163
Tomato Sauce	Page 167
Green Sauce	Page 168
Bolognese Ragù	Page 169
Basil Pesto	Page 170

Celery and Macadamia Pesto   Page 171
Mayonnaise   Page 172
Bechamel   Page 173
Ratatouille   Page 177
Celery root coleslaw   Page 178
Pickled onions   Page 179
Roasted bell peppers   Page 180
Black rice with lemon   Page 181
Sautéd Mushrooms   Page 182
Fennel au gratin   Page 183
Abbreviations & Conversions   Page 185
Notes   Page 186

APPETIZERS

Zucchini Galette	Page	19
Eggplant towers	Page	21
Frittata with zucchini	Page	23
Focaccia	Page	25
Tomato, Mozzarella and Egg	Page	27
Russian Salad	Page	28

Zucchini Galette

A rustic, flaky tart

A V B Gf Ef

---

 30 Minutes   4 People

Ingredients

---

1 sheet of gluten-free puff pastry
6 zucchini
2 cloves of garlic
2 Tbsp. Evoo
2 Tbsp. vegetarian egg replacer
4 Tbsp. water
2 Tbsp. organic heavy whipping cream
4 oz. of creamy goat cheese
1 Tbsp. mint leaves, minced
Salt
Pepper

Directions

Preheat the over to 420 F. Wash and dry the zucchini. Remove and discard the two ends, then cut into thin rounds. Peel the garlic, cut in half and sauté in the Evoo. When the garlic starts turning golden, add the zucchini, salt and pepper, and sauté until cooked but not soft, about 10 minutes, stirring often. Remove the garlic and stir in the minced mint.
While the zucchini are cooking, in a big bowl mix the egg replacer with 4 Tbsp. of water and the cream. Add the zucchini and stir to blend the ingredients.
Cut a piece of parchment paper, sprinkle it with a little flour and roll the dough directly on the paper, until it's 11 inches in diameter. Transfer the rolled dough into a 9-inch non-stick quiche pan by holding the corners of the parchment paper. Fill the dough with the zucchini mix and fold the sides of the dough over the filling. Bake until the dough turns golden, about 20 minutes.
Cut the goat cheese into small dollops and put them on the quiche when it's still hot.
Cut into slices and serve warm.

Eggplant towers

A fancy variation of eggplant Parmigiana

Sr V B Gf Ef

---

 60 Minutes   4 People

Ingredients

2 big eggplants
4 ripe round tomatoes
5 Tbsp. of extra virgin olive oil
Basil, approx. 30 leaves
4 Tbsp. crumbled feta cheese
Salt

Directions

Peel the eggplant and cut it into rounds 1/3 inch thick (you will need 16 slices). Lay them on a paper towel, sprinkle with salt and let sit for at least 20 minutes. You'll notice that after a few minutes the eggplant start "oozing" a brown liquid. Remove it with a paper towel and lay four slices of eggplant on an oven pan covered with parchment paper with Evoo.
Wash the tomatoes and slice them into rounds 1/3 inch thick. Remove the basil leaves from the stems and wash them.
Put one slice of tomato on top of each eggplant round, then ½ Tbsp. of crumbled feta cheese, a few drops of Evoo, some salt, and 2 basil leaves. Make one more layer in the same order. Cook in the oven for 20-25 minutes at 400F. Put a fresh basil leaf on top of each tower and serve warm or cold.

Frittata with zucchini

A versatile appetizer

Sr V B Gf Ef

 40 Minutes   4 People

Ingredients

6 eggs, fresh and organic
2 medium zucchini
½ red onion
4 slices of cooked ham
1 Tbsp. of parsley, chopped
4 Tbsp. Evoo
Salt
Pepper

Directions

Wash and dry the zucchini. Cut and discard the two tips, then cut in rounds approx. ¼ inch thick. Chop the onion and sauté in 2 Tbsp. of Evoo. When the onion starts turning translucent, add the zucchini, the ham, salt and pepper, and sauté until cooked but not soft, about 7 minutes.
Break the eggs into a mixing bowl, add a pinch of salt and beat with an electric beater at high speed for about 3 minutes. Add the cooked zucchini to the eggs, clean the pan with a paper towel and grease it with 1 Tbsp. Evoo. Warm up the pan and pour the eggs & zucchini mix into the pan, spreading the zucchini evenly.
With a non-stick spatula, keep pushing the rim of the frittata towards its center, so that the rest of the eggs come into contact with the hot pan. Keeping the heat on medium/high, repeat this operation all around the frittata. Make sure it doesn't stick to the bottom of the pan by sliding the spatula under its rim.
Flip the frittata. For this tricky maneuver I prefer to warm up a second pan, slightly bigger than the first one. I grease it with oil, making sure it's very warm before transferring the frittata into it. Then I move over the sink – absolutely do not do it over the stove! – to flip my frittata into the second pan. It takes guts but it can be done.
If you have only one pan, flip the frittata onto a flat platter, then carefully slide it back into the pan.
Again, push the edge of the frittata away from the rim of the pan and make sure it doesn't stick to the bottom by raising it with the spatula. If the frittata lost its round shape when you flipped it, push it back together with the spatula. Cover with a lid and cook for 3 to 4 minutes on low heat. Transfer the frittata onto a plate and serve warm or cold.

Focaccia

Something everyone likes

A V Ef

---

 40 Minutes + raising time

 4 People

Ingredients

---

300 g. all-purpose flour
100 g. bread flour
300 ml. water
6 g. of fresh yeast (or
3 g. of instant yeast)
9 g. salt
Crystal salt for the top
2 sprigs of rosemary
2 Tbsp. Evoo + 1 for greasing
the baking pan

Tip: If you cannot stay at home for the whole time it takes to make the dough, you can put the dough in the refrigerator 24 hours. Just remember to take it out at least one hour before baking it.

Directions

Warm up the water to 90-95 F, pour it into a big bowl and dissolve the yeast.
Add the flour and stir with a spoon. After all flour has been absorbed, add the salt and keep mixing. At this stage the dough will look sticky and messy but don't worry, it will come together. Cover the bowl with plastic film and let it rest for 15 minutes.
**After the 15 minutes, transfer the dough onto a lightly floured surface, put some flour on your hands and fold it as follows: think of a compass and grab the east side of the dough with both hands, pull it gently and fold it over the center of the dough. Repeat with the north side of the dough, then the east side, and after doing it with the south side flip the dough upside down. Return the dough to the bowl, cover, and let it rest for 15 minutes.
Repeat from ** to ** two more times (for a total of 45 minutes)
After the three foldings, make the dough into a ball let it rise for approx. 2 hours or until it doubles in size.
Oil well the bottom of the baking pan, then flatten the dough with oiled fingertips directly in the baking pan. Keep flattening the dough with your fingertips until you get the desired size.
Cover it with plastic film and let it rise in a warm place for 1 hour.
Warm up the oven at 400 F.
With a fork, make a few holes on the surface of the focaccia. Brush evenly 2 Tbsp. of Evoo on the dough and grind some coarse salt on top. Remove the leaves from the rosemary stem and arrange them on the dough.
Bake until golden, approx. 20-25 minutes.

Tomato, Mozzarella and Egg

A refreshing meal starter

Sp Sr V B Gf

---

 20 Minutes   4 People

Ingredients

---

2 big ripe organic tomatoes
3 Tbsp. organic mayonnaise
(see my recipe)
3 hard boiled organic eggs
2 balls of fresh mozzarella
20-25 leaves of basil
3 Tbsp. Evoo
Black salt

Directions

Put the eggs in a small saucepan filled with cold water and cook them for eight minutes, counting from when the water starts to boil.
Wash and dry the tomatoes and cut them in round slices ¼ inch thick.
Arrange the tomatoes on a serving plate, salt them, and then spread a teaspoon of mayonnaise on each of them.
Slice the mozzarella into 1/3-inch thick rounds and place them over the tomato slices. Insert a leaf or two of basil between the tomato and the mozzarella.
Peel the eggs and cut them into rounds with a knife or with an egg slicer.
Place the egg slices over the mozzarella.
Put a few basil leaves in a mortar, pour the oil over them and crush with the pestle until the oil turns green.
Drizzle with this basil-infused oil and
serve cold.

Russian Salad

A timeless appetizer

A B V Gf Df

 40 Minutes   4 People

Ingredients

3 medium potatoes
3 carrots
8 oz. of shelled green peas
2 eggs
1 Tbsp of apple cider vinegar
2 Tbsp. Evoo
2 Tbsp. mayonnaise* (see recipe)
Salt
Pepper

Directions

Boil the eggs and let them cool down. Wash and peel the potatoes and the carrots. Dice them into 1/4-inch cubes, and either steam them or boil them separately in salted water. It will only take a few minutes because they must be firm but not mushy.
Boil or steam the green peas in water until tender.
Spread the veggies on a platter to cool down, otherwise they will add moisture to your salad.
In a mixing bowl, dress the three vegetables with the vinegar and oil, dice the eggs, add them to the veggie mix, and delicately toss together with 2 Tbsp. of mayonnaise*.
Serve cold.

* If you are allergic to eggs or prefer a lighter version of this recipe, replace the mayonnaise with 3 Tbsp. of plain yogurt and omit the eggs.

Variety

The other day, while waiting in line at the cash register after shopping for groceries, I double-checked my list and my cart for the usual two reasons: to verify that I had bought everything and to make sure that there was enough variety.

I love variety, not only because I know that it's an excellent dietary habit but also because it affords me the luxury of being creative with my menus and satisfying my eating whims.

I've been this way since I can remember. When my mother sent me to the grocery store with a list of things to buy, I regularly came home with two or three extra items "just in case," like I used to tell her to justify my digressions from her precise instructions. My purchases didn't reflect the typical desires of a girl of my age (ice cream, candies, chips, etc.) but were instead simple alternatives to what my mother was usually cooking.

Although my mother was a great cook, she was repetitive. She never admitted her creativity limitations, she never bought cookbooks for inspiration, and therefore her cooking ended up being monotonous. She cooked way too much meat for my taste but, every time I dared to complain, she threatened, "If you don't like what I cook, you can ask my friend Lina to adopt you!" She knew all too well that such a prospect would quickly put an end to my grumbles, and it regularly worked.

My mother's friend Lina got married very young, knowing very little about cooking. One of the first things she understood about her culinary duties was that she didn't like learning, shopping, and planning involved.

She found and implemented a straightforward solution: she decided that she would learn to cook fourteen different dishes and cook the same two (one for lunch and one for dinner) on the same day of the week.

I remember her husband joking that he didn't need a calendar to know the day of the week. All he had to do was look at his plate because for the fifty-plus years they were married, Lina kept serving exactly the same two dishes on the same day of the week.

And she didn't even put effort into making them special in any way. One would

expect that she would produce wonderful pasta, or rich pot-roasts, or creamy risottos and hearty soups with all that practice. Instead, everything she made had a bland taste, still acceptable, but in an anonymous, dull way.

Even physically, Lina wasn't the archetype of the Italian cook: tall, stern, and bony, she reflected the frugality of her table or vice versa. My mother knew very well how much I disliked Lina's hospital-style, repetitive cuisine. She did as well because she always found a pretext – while pinching my arm so I wouldn't dare to expose her fib – not to accept her friend's rare invitations to dinner.

It's well known that the little and big traumas of our childhood end up guiding our choices as adults, so I guess that Lina's culinary monotony is one of the reasons why I love diversity so much.

Combine that with my habit of planning my menus according to the weather – I hate the idea of a salad on a cold day as much as I find a hot soup unpleasant in the summer – and you'll find me checking the weekly weather forecast before doing my grocery shopping.

Not a bad idea, you must admit.

I can still improvise, but it's reassuring to have all the ingredients I need so that most of the menus are already basted in my mind at the beginning of the week, and I can devote more attention to the fine stitching, i.e., the little surprises that can make any meal unique, innovative, and more enjoyable.

So I encourage you to buy a special bread, a couple of extra different vegetables, those tiny greens that go on everything, or a type of cheese you've never tried before.

Go to the produce section of your supermarket or your Farmers' Market, close your eyes for a second and imagine the tastes of what is in front of you. Decide what your heart desires and, with generosity and imagination, try to envision it on your table. Be daring with new tastes, experiment with different combinations, and be creative.

It's not going to make a big difference on your budget, but it's certainly going to have a big impact on your mood, health, and the way you think of food.

We are lucky that so many choices are available to us; let's take advantage of them!

SALADS

Pantesca salad   Page   37
Tuna and Cannellini Salad   Page   39
Carrot Salad   Page   41
Radicchio Orange and Fennel   Page   43
Celery Root Salad   Page   45
Belgian Endive and Fennel   Page   47
Chicken Salad   Page   49
Fennel, Beet and Goat Cheese   Page   51

Pantesca salad

An amazing salad from Pantelleria Island

S B Gf Df Ef V

 30 Minutes   4 People

Ingredients

3 Yukon gold potatoes
1 lb. ripe red tomatoes
2 Tbsp. capers in vinegar
2 oz. pitted green olives
1/2 red sweet onion
1 pinch of dried oregano
A few leaves of fresh basil
5 Tbsp. Evoo
2 Tbsp. red wine vinegar
Salt & pepper to taste

Directions

Wash the potatoes and peel them, cut into cubes and steam until cooked but still firm (8-10 minutes).
Peel the half onion and slice it thinly.
Wash and cut the tomatoes into big pieces.
Put these first three ingredients into a serving bowl, add the olives, the capers, the washed basil, and the oregano.
Prepare the dressing in a small bowl: mix the olive oil, the red vinegar, salt and pepper and whisk with a fork.
Pour the dressing over the salad, toss gently and serve.

Tuna and Cannellini Salad

Crunchy and nutritious

A B Gf Ef Df

---

 15 Minutes   4 People

Ingredients

10 oz. of canned tuna
3 stalks of celery
1 yellow bell pepper
1 can of cannellini beans
25-30 green olives
Pickled onions (see recipe)
4 Tbsp. of Evoo
Salt & Pepper to taste

Directions

Wash, dry and dice the bell pepper and celery. Rinse the cannellini beans under running water. Combine these ingredients with the canned tuna in a bowl, add the olives, dress with Evoo, salt and pepper, and toss.
Arrange on serving plates, and top with some pickled onions (see my recipe).

Carrot Salad

So easy yet so tasty

Sp V B Df Ef Gf

---

 15 Minutes   4 People

Ingredients

6 organic carrots
3 Tbsp. of Evoo
1 lemon
½ cup of raisins
¼ cup roasted pine nuts
Salt
Pepper
a few curls of lemon rind

Directions

Soak the raisins in a cup of warm water for 15 minutes. Meanwhile, wash and peel the carrots with a potato peeler, cut them into big pieces and julienne them.
Roast the pine nuts in a small pan and set aside.
Squeeze the lemon, mix it with Evoo, salt and pepper.
Drain the raisins, pat them dry with a paper towel, and add them to the carrots, together with the roasted pine nuts. Pour the dressing on the carrots, and toss. Garnish with a few curls of lemon rind and serve.

Radicchio Orange and Fennel

A colorful winter salad

W V B Gf Ef Df

---

 20 Minutes   4 People

Ingredients

1 head of round red radicchio
2 big oranges
sweet anise (aka fennel)
2 Tbsp. of balsamic vinegar
6 Tbsp. Evoo
Salt

Directions

Wash, dry, and cut in half the radicchio and slice it very thin. Arrange it in the center of the serving dishes. Cut and discard the green part of the fennel, keeping the fine green leaves for garnishing. Wash the white part and slice it thinly. Arrange it around the radicchio.
Peel the orange with a sharp knife, removing also all the white skin. Pull out the sections from in-between the skin and arrange them on the radicchio.
Garnish your salad with the fennel green leaves.
In a small bowl, mix the balsamic vinegar, Evoo and salt; pour a couple of tablespoons on each salad.

Celery Root Salad

When creativity meets originality

W V B Gf Ef

---

 20 Minutes   4 People

Ingredients

1 celery root
3 Tbsp. of Evoo
1 lemon
2 oz. of Parmesan or Pecorino, shaved
salt
pepper

Directions

Peel the celery root with a potato peeler, cut it in quarters and slice it thinly with the potato peeler.
Squeeze the lemon, pour it on the sliced celery root and toss.
Wash the central, tender leaves of the celery root, dry them, chop them finely and add them to your salad.
Shave the cheese on top of the celery; add salt, pepper, Evoo, and serve.

Belgian Endive and Fennel

An innovative winter salad

W F V B Gf Df Ef

---

 20 Minutes   4 People

Ingredients

2 heads of green Belgian endive
2 heads of red Belgian endive
1 bulb of fennel
½ cup of pine nuts
1 oz. of aged pecorino cheese
2 Tbsp. of champagne vinegar
3 Tbsp. of Evoo
Himalayan salt to taste

Directions

Roast the pine nuts in a small skillet, stirring often until golden brown. Remove from skillet immediately and let cool down. Wash the Belgian endive, discard the external leaves, and cut it thinly.

Wash the fennel bulb, discard the hard external layer and the green stalks but save some of the feathery green leaves for garnishing. Cut the fennel in half and slice it very thinly, either with a knife or with a mandolin.

Prepare the dressing by mixing oil, vinegar and salt in a small bowl. Transfer veggies into a salad bowl, add toasted pine nuts, add dressing, and toss. Slice the pecorino cheese with a vegetable peeler and serve.

Chicken Salad

An inviting and versatile dish

A B Gf Df

---

 60 Minutes   4 People

Ingredients

The meat from half roasted chicken
or 1 lb. of organic chicken breast
1 carrot (optional)
1 stalk of celery (optional)
half yellow onion (optional)
1 Tbsp. of EVOO
2 tender stalks of celery
1 yellow bell pepper
a handful of roasted pumpkin seeds
the juice of half lemon
Salt
2 Tbsp. of mayonnaise (see my recipe)

Directions

If you don't have any chicken leftovers, boil the chicken breast until tender (approximately 40 minutes) in a quart of water, together with half yellow onion, one carrot and one stalk of celery. In the meantime, make the mayonnaise (see my recipe). Then wash and peel the carrot, wash the celery and the bell pepper. Chop finely the celery and the carrot, cut the bell pepper into thin slices removing the seeds and white membrane inside, and then dice them. Mince the chicken, put it into a mixing bowl, squeeze the lemon on top of it, toss, add the chopped vegetables, the roasted pumpkin seeds, the mayonnaise, toss again and serve.

N.B. Please remember to wash your hands and every surface that has been in touch with the chicken with hot water and anti-bacterial soap since poultry meat is very prone to contamination by the dangerous bacterium E. coli.

Fennel, Beet and Goat Cheese

The ultimate winter salad

W V B Gf Ef

---

 60 Minutes   4 People

Ingredients

One bunch of green lettuce
1 sweet anise
2 red beets
1 cup of roasted hazelnuts
1 Tbsp. of balsamic vinegar
8 Tbsp. EVOO
Himalayan salt

Directions

Wash the beets and boil them in water until firm, about 40 minutes. Let them cool down while you prepare the other ingredients.
Was the lettuce and dry it in the salad spinner.
Cut and discard the green part of the fennel, wash the white part and slice it thinly.
Roast the hazelnuts in a pan or in the oven.
Peel and cut the beets.
Arrange these ingredients on serving plates, then cut the goat cheese into small bites and lay some on top of each salad.
In a small bowl, mix the balsamic vinegar, EVOO and salt; pour a couple of tablespoons over each salad and serve.

With a grain of salt

One day a dear friend of mine was waiting for her delayed flight when, as it often happens in these situations, she started to chat with another passenger.

Noticing his accent, my friend – a gourmand who owns a beautiful restaurant in Napa – asked if he was from "down under."

The man was indeed Australian, and when he said that he came from "the Murray River area," my friend exclaimed, "I know precisely where it is!"

"I betcha you do, mate!" the Aussie replied, giving her a skeptical look.

"No, I really do! It's where my favorite salt comes from!"

"Oh, yeah, we had all that salt we wanted to get rid of, but nobody wanted to buy it. So one day, we decided to market it at a ridiculously high price, and now it sells like hotcakes!"

Of course, my friends thought that the Australian was joking, but thinking of another story that my mother told me many years ago, his marketing strategy made sense.

After World War II, my maternal grandfather – who owned a small farm near Padua, Italy – wanted to get rid of a big pile of manure that he had no use for. After having tried to sell it for a while, he had to resign himself to give it away for free. Still, nobody wanted it. He even volunteered to cart it to anyone who could use it, but again nobody seemed interested.

The summer was approaching, and he needed to do something about the stinking pile.

He had noticed that – after the arrival of the American Army in Italy – anything that came in a box or a can had become extremely popular, regardless of the quality of the product. So my grandfather made a deal with a local cannery: if they agreed to put his manure in cans, he would split the revenues fifty-fifty with them.

What did the trick was his marketing strategy. He labeled the cans "Ematel – The new American super-fertilizer. Wonderful for your roses and your geraniums" and asked a garden supply store – catering to the downtown ladies – to sell a sample lot of cans. The first batch sold out so quickly that the canning

company couldn't keep up with the demand. The buyers never realized that Ematel is the Italian word for manure (letame) spelled backward.

Please forgive me for putting salt and manure in the same story, a little disrespectful towards such a precious commodity as salt has always been throughout human history.

Because of its use in preserving food when refrigeration was not available, many wars have been fought to control salt mines and salt routes. Salt has been used as currency and often traded ounce for ounce for gold. Until a few decades ago, it was such a significant source of tax revenues for many countries that the people caught using seawater for cooking were fined or imprisoned.

Then, thanks to better extraction techniques and cheaper transportation, salt has slowly become less and less expensive and more widely available.

Recently new types of salt have made their appearance on the culinary scene, and salt has become, once again, expensive. For being just salt, I mean.

I must admit that I was a little skeptical about spending so much money on sodium chloride just because it came from a far corner of the planet. After all, sodium chloride is sodium chloride, no matter how big or small or colorful its grains are.

However, after doing some research and trying different kinds of salt, I must admit that my "salt is salt" belief was wrong.

To my defense, I have to say that I grew up in a place and in a time when salt was a state monopoly, sold only at tobacconists (yes, you read right). It was strictly white and came in two forms: coarse (used to preserve food and salt the water for cooking pasta) and fine (for all the other cooking purposes).

Growing up in Italy, I have seen many salt works, and the salt-making process seemed so straightforward that I trusted the product to be pure: let the seawater evaporate, harvest, clean impurities, package, and sell.

However, during my research, I found out that salt is no longer what it used to be (or I believed it was). Most table salts go through a process that removes beneficial minerals and adds anti-caking agents and preservatives. Couldn't we keep adding some rice grains to the shaker so that the salt didn't cake? Did I want to keep cooking with such processed salts?

So I decided to experiment with the new ones available on the market, but I first needed to understand more about them with so much choice.

Salt falls into three categories:

Sea Salt is made from the evaporation of seawater and available in fine grains or larger crystals.

Rock salt is a mineral derived from sodium chloride; it's found in underground deposits.

Kosher salt comes from either seawater or underground salt mines, but it doesn't contain any preservatives. It takes its name from its use in the koshering process.

All three of them serve their purposes: enhancing the taste of food, pickling, preserving, braining, adding iodine to our diet, frosting our margarita glasses, and, unfortunately, raising our blood pressure.

Then there is a great variety of gourmet salts that do the same things, plus adding very subtle but distinct flavors to our recipes. They come in an array of pale nuances that range from black to grey, to pink, to taupe, to snowy white, and in various textures that go from superfine to coarse to slabs on which you can cook.

Unlike your ordinary table salts, though, they don't simply exalt flavors: they add texture, surprise, even sexiness to your food. What a delight to find that unexpected little grain that melts on your tongue, tingling not only your taste but also other senses, suddenly reminding you of that wonderful vacation on the beach! And what to say of the tanginess that those tiny Himalayan gems put in all your salads? And the smokiness you can add to your fish and meats with just a few flakes of Murray salt?

As you might have guessed, it took a grain of it to admit and overcome my prejudices, but then I fell in love with salt!

Here are some of your delightful choices. Try some of them until you find your favorites. They might seem pricey, but they last a long time, and you only need to use them sparingly. Please get in the habit of alternating them since each one contains different minerals that are very beneficial.

Himalayan Pink: rock salt from India and Pakistan.

Bolivian rose: rock salt from the Bolivian Andes

Gris de Guerande: grey sea salt from Brittany, France.

Murray River: rock salt from North West Victoria, Australia

Maldon: sea salt flakes from England. It also comes in a smoked variety.

Kala Namak: also called Black Salt, it's actually a purplish-grey rock salt from India.

Trapani white: sea salt from the Mediterranean coast of Sicily

Cervia Sweet Salt: sea salt from the Adriatic coast of Italy

Alea Sea Salt: sea salt from Hawai'i

Black Lava: sea salt from Hawai'i

PASTA, ETC.

Fettuccine with basil pesto   Page   59
Orecchiette with broccoli rabe   Page   61
Zucchini Spaghetti   Page   63
Roman Gnocchi   Page   65
Polenta   Page   67
Pizza! Pizza!   Page   68
Pizza Margherita   Page   73
Asparagus Risotto   Page   77
Riso and Zucca   Page   79
Mushroom Risotto   Page   81
Rice and Green Peas   Page   83
Chickpea soup   Page   85
Squash soup   Page   87
White beans and rice soup   Page   89

Fettuccine with basil pesto

A dish that makes you dream of the Italian Riviera

Sp Sr V B

---

 40 Minutes   4 People

Ingredients

8 oz. of egg pasta like fettuccine
2 medium yellow organic potatoes
½ lb. organic green beans
2 tsp. Kosher salt
½ oz. of Parmesan cheese
a handful of pine nuts

For the pesto sauce:

25-30 leaves of fresh basil
2 Tbsp. of pine nuts
4-5 Tablespoons of Evoo
½ oz. of pecorino cheese
½ oz. of Parmesan cheese

Directions

Make the pesto sauce.
Wash the basil and remove the leaves from the stems. Combine 1 Tbsp. of pine nuts (reserve the other Tbsp. for later) the Evoo, the pecorino cheese, the Parmesan cheese and 20 leaves of basil (reserve the other 5 for later) in the blender, olive oil first. Start on low and slowly increase the speed. If the ingredients don't blend well, add more olive oil or one tablespoon of water. The result should be a smooth, light-green sauce.
Trim and wash the green beans, and cut them into ½ inch pieces.
Peel the potatoes and cut them into ½ inch cubes.
Bring 3 quarts of water to a full boil. Add the salt, the pasta, the green beans and the potatoes. Cook al dente, according to the pasta package directions. While the pasta is cooking, take 2 Tbsp. of the water into which it's cooking and add them to the pesto, stirring.
Drain the pasta, green beans and potatoes, transfer into a serving bowl, dress with the pesto sauce, toss well and decorate with the remaining pine nuts and basil leaves, shredded with your hands. Grate some Parmesan cheese on top and serve.

Orecchiette with broccoli rabe

A flavorful durum semolina pasta from Apulia

A   B   Ef

 40 Minutes   4 People

Ingredients

10 oz. of orecchiette pasta
1 lb. of broccoli rabe (rapini)
Four to six quarts of cold water
6 Tbsp. of extra virgin olive oil
10 canned anchovies
1 oz. grated Pecorino cheese
A few flakes of red pepper
2 Tbsp. of bread crumbs
2 tsp. of salt

Directions

Put the water to boil, in a pot big enough to cook the first two ingredients. Don't be deceived by the amount of broccoli rabe as they will significantly decrease after cooking.

Cut off and discard the tough ends of the broccoli rabe, wash them thoroughly and cut them into 2-inch pieces. As soon as the water reaches a full, rolling boil, add first the salt and then the pasta. Gently stir and after three minutes add the broccoli rabe. While the pasta is cooking, warm up 4 Tbsp. of oil in a saucepan and cook the anchovies until they melt.

In a separate pan, toast the bread crumbs with 2 Tbsp. of Evoo. When the pasta is cooked al dente (follow package directions for cooking time), drain the pasta and broccoli rabe, transfer them into a serving bowl, dress with the anchovies & oil mix, grated Pecorino cheese, red pepper, toasted breadcrumbs, toss and serve hot.

Zucchini Spaghetti

It doesn't get more vegetarian than this!

A V B Gf Ef

 20 Minutes   4 People

Ingredients

6 medium organic zucchini
3 Tbsp. Evoo
4 tsp. of grated pecorino cheese
12-16 leaves of basil
8 oz. of tomato sauce (see my recipe)
Salt

Directions

Make the tomato sauce according to the recipe or, if you already have it frozen or canned, warm it up with the remaining 2 Tbsp. of Evoo and salt. Wash and dry the zucchini. Remove and discard the ends and, with a spiralizer, make them into long, spaghetti-like ribbons. Sauté the zucchini spaghetti in 1 Tbsp. of Evoo for 5-7 minutes, stirring often. Add salt to taste. Divide the zucchini onto 4 serving dishes, dress with sauce and basil leaves, sprinkle with grated cheese, and serve warm.

Roman Gnocchi

A heavenly first course

🕐 60 Minutes +
cooling time

👤 6 People

Ingredients

2 cups of semolina flour
1 quart of organic milk
1 cup of grated Parmesan cheese
1 cup of unsalted organic butter + 1 Tbsp.
for the oven pan
2 egg yolks
Salt

Directions

Pour the milk into a saucepan, add a big pinch of salt and bring to a boil.

Lower the heat and start adding the semolina flour, little by little, stirring vigorously with a whisk to avoid forming any lumps; cook for ten minutes on low heat stirring constantly with a wooden spoon because this mixture will become very thick and stick to the bottom of the saucepan. Remove the saucepan from the stovetop and incorporate, stirring vigorously, ½ cup of butter, 3 Tbsp. of grated Parmesan cheese and, one at a time, the two egg yolks.

When everything is well blended and smooth, wet the bottom of a baking pan with cold water and pour this mixture on it, spreading it with a spatula to a half-inch thickness.

Let this mixture sit for two hours, until completely cooled down and firm, and then cut it into rounds with a molding ring.

Preheat the oven to 400 F.

Grease casserole with some butter and arrange the semolina rounds in rows, slightly overlapping them.

Cut the remaining ½ cup of butter into small cubes, scatter them over the semolina squares and dust with the remaining grated Parmesan cheese.

Cook in the oven for about 30 minutes or until the top turns golden-brown.

Serve warm.

Polenta

A northern Italian creamy dish with cornmeal

F W V B Gf Df Ef

 70 Minutes

 4 People

Ingredients

2 ½ cups of yellow corn meal
6 cups of water
2 tsp. of salt
1 Tbsp of Evoo

Directions

Bring the water to a boil in a pot, lower the heat, add the salt, the oil, and gradually add the cornmeal, stirring with a whisk to avoid forming any lumps.

The mix will look runny, but don't be deceived because it will thicken as it cooks.

Cook for at least 50 minutes, uncovered and stirring as often as possible. It's normal that the bottom part gets burned and sticks to the pot. This will give your polenta a nice smoky taste without ruining the pot. Simply soak the pot overnight in cold water and the crust will soften, to be easily removed.

Serve with meat or vegetable stews, cheese, or sautéd mushrooms.

Pizza! Pizza!

Yes, Pizza with capital P and exclamation marks because it is my absolute favorite food.

This amazing savory pie is very simple in its ingredients and yet so hard to replicate in the traditional way. Hard because you need the right ingredients – amazingly, just a handful – but they must be the right ones: Water, salt, yeast, and flour for the dough, fresh mozzarella, tomatoes, basil, or oregano for the topping.

Sounds pretty simple, doesn't it? But the crucial component to obtaining a great pizza is the oven. According to the AVPN (the True Neapolitan Pizza Association), "the cooking must be done exclusively in a wood-fired oven, which has reached a temperature between 430-480C°. With these temperatures, just insert the pizza for 60-90 seconds. The pizza will cook evenly across the entire circumference."

Of course – or unfortunately – there are hundreds of variations of the original recipe – deep dish, thin crust, endless choice of toppings, cheesy crust, even baked in the barbecue – but for me, the only pizza remains the Pizza Napoletana Verace, the True Neapolitan Pizza.

The AVPN is a non-profit organization founded in 1984 in Naples. Its mission is to promote and protect the authentic Neapolitan pizza, made in accordance with the characteristics described in the AVPN International Regulations in Italy and worldwide.

Just a brief look at the Association's method of production – a 14-page document called Disciplinare – will give you an idea of how important it has become to preserve the authenticity of pizza, not only in Naples but all over the world.

The Disciplinare regulates everything: from the type of flour to be used to the pH of water, from the duration of the dough rising (called fermentation) to the weight of the dough balls (panetti), the diameter of the pizza, the three variations of tomatoes and two certified kinds of mozzarella.

Most importantly, the AVPN recognizes only two types of Pizza: 'Marinara' (tomato, oil, oregano, and garlic) and 'Margherita' (tomato, oil, mozzarella or fior di latte, grated pecorino cheese and basil).

If you have heard that Pizza Margherita was named after a queen, I believe that

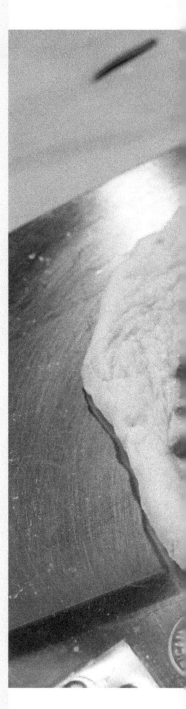

the story is true because Margherita of Savoy wasn't the typical queen of her time. She traveled all over Italy on her husband's behalf with the scope of making popular the royal house of the recently united country, which she achieved thanks to her ability to show her genuine enthusiasm for local customs, traditions, and culture. She was particularly fond of Naples, her first residence, and the town where her only child was born. I can easily picture her going to eat the local food and why a very honored pizzaiolo decided to name a pizza after his queen. Hosting royalty was a rare event to be remembered for generations, and it's easy to make the connection between the colors of the popular food and those of the Italian flag: red tomatoes, green basil, and white cheese.

A wood-fired oven remains one of my dreams, but I have learned a few tricks to make a good pizza at home over the years.

I have bought a high-quality pizza stone that mimics the base of a wood-fired oven and gives my pizza a nice crust. I make my tomato sauce. I use only fresh buffalo mozzarella, fresh basil, and cold-pressed organic extra-virgin Italian olive oil.

Despite all my efforts, I must admit that no pizza I've ever made compares to a True Neapolitan Pizza eaten in Naples. Some people say it's the flour. Others swear it's the local water. Others maintain it's the sea air that makes it unique. I believe it's a combination of all these factors plus the tomatoes grown in volcanic soil, the freshness of local mozzarella, the wood they use in the oven, but mainly the skills of the pizzaioli, refined and perfected over centuries of baking their acclaimed and unique pizza.

Pizza Margherita

The Queen of Pizzas

A V Ef

I have tried many different recipes and methods to make pizza at home, but I keep going back to the one by Alessandro Servidio. Making the dough is easy, it doesn't require a mixer, and the result is excellent. It uses a modified autolyse technique that doesn't require kneading. Try this method and you'll love it like me.

 70 Minutes + raising time

 4 - 6 People

Ingredients

---

400 g. all-purpose flour
 100 g. bread flour
350 ml. water
6 g. of fresh yeast or 3 g. of instant yeast
12 g. salt
½ pint tomato sauce (see recipe)
1 buffalo mozzarella
A few leaves of basil
1 Tbsp. of Evoo

Directions

Measure the first six ingredients before starting.

Warm up the water to 90-95 F, pour it into a big bowl and dissolve the yeast.

Add the flour and mix with a spoon. After all the flour has been absorbed, add the salt and keep mixing. At this stage the dough will look sticky and messy, but don't worry, it will come together. Cover the bowl with plastic film and let it rest for 15 minutes.

**After the 15 minutes, transfer the dough onto a lightly floured surface, put some flour on your hands and fold it as follows: think of a compass and grab the east side of the dough with both hands, pull it gently and fold it over the center of the dough. Repeat with the north side of the dough, then the east side, and after doing it with the south side flip the dough upside down. Return the dough to the bowl, cover, and let it rest for 15 minutes. **

Repeat from ** to ** two more times (for a total of 45 minutes)

First fermentation: After the three foldings, let the dough rise for approx. 2 hours or until it doubles in size.

Second Fermentation: Divide the dough into two parts, fold them again, and close them at the base to form two balls (panetti). Let the panetti rise for approx. 2 hours or until they double in size. I put them on an oiled

baking sheet and cover them loosely (since they are going to double) with plastic film.

Warm up the oven to 500 F well in advance, especially if you have a pizza stone. This way your oven will be uniformly warm.

Shape your pizzas on a floured surface, one at a time. Flatten the dough with your fingertips, starting from the center and moving outwards, to form the cornicione, the typical raised edge. Keep flattening the dough with your fingertips until you reach the desired size.

If you have a pizza stone and a peel, transfer the dough to the floured peel and put the condiments on the pizza. Otherwise, put the dough on a pizza dish.

Spread the tomato sauce starting from the middle and moving outwards, with a circular motion.

Add the mozzarella, a few drops of olive oil, basil, and bake until the crust turns golden brown.

Asparagus Risotto

A favorite spring recipe

Sp V B Gf Ef

 30 Minutes

 4 People

Ingredients

10 – 12 spears of organic green asparagus
10 oz. of rice (Arborio or Carnaroli)
A pot of boiling water
2 Tbsp. of butter
3 Tbsp. of Evoo
1 organic bouillon cube
½ yellow onion, chopped
3 Tbsp. of grated Parmesan cheese

Directions

Wash the asparagus, cut and discard the hard ends, then cut them into ½ inch-long sections, setting aside the tips. Peel the onion and chop it finely. Grate the Parmesan cheese and set aside. Sauté the onion with the oil and half the butter, on medium heat, until slightly golden. Raise the heat, add the bouillon cube and let it melt – always stirring – then add the asparagus sections. Cook for one minute.

Add the rice and let it toast on high heat – always stirring – for a couple of minutes, until the grains look translucent. This passage is very important because the rice must absorb the fat, so that it doesn't absorb too much liquid while cooking and the grains remain separated.

Add 1 cup of hot water, stir the rice, and lower the heat to medium-low. When the risotto starts to thicken, add some hot water, one ladle at a time, stirring often.

It usually takes between 12 and 15 minutes for the rice to cook. Taste it after 10 minutes and, when it looks almost done, add the asparagus tips, adjust for salt if needed, add half a ladle of hot water, stir, remove from the stove and let it sit – covered – for a couple of minutes. Uncover, add the rest of the butter and the Parmesan cheese, stir and serve immediately as it tends to thicken very quickly.

Riso and Zucca

A creamy squash risotto

F W B Gf Ef V

---

 40 Minutes   4 People

Ingredients

½ Kabocha or 1 acorn squash
10 oz. of rice (Arborio or Carnaroli)
1/2 Tbsp. of butter
3 Tbsp. of olive oil
1 tsp. of organic beef base
½ yellow onion, chopped
3 tablespoons of grated Parmesan cheese
1 pot of boiling water
Some minced parsley for garnishing

Directions

Cut the squash into quarters – be careful, it's quite hard – remove the seeds, and peel the green skin it with a potato peeler. Cut it into ½ inch cubes.

Peel the onion and chop it finely.

Grate the Parmesan cheese and set aside. Sauté the onion with the oil and butter, on medium heat, until slightly golden. Raise the heat; add the squash cubes, the beef base, and a couple of ladles of hot water.

Stir, lower the heat to medium, cover and cook for 15 minutes.

Blend until creamy with an immersion blender, bring back to a boil and add the rice, stirring often and adding hot water to prevent it from thickening.

It usually takes between 12 and 15 minutes for the rice to cook. Taste it after 10 minutes and, when it looks almost done, adjust for salt if needed, add half a ladle of water, turn off the heat and let it sit – covered – for a couple of minutes. Serve in bowls, sprinkling with Parmesan cheese, minced parsley, and a few drops of olive oil.

Tip 1: you will only need half Kabocha squash. Cut the other half into cubes and freeze them.

Tip 2: If you need some extra warmth, grate some fresh ginger on top of each dish

Mushroom Risotto

One of the tastier risottos, guaranteed to become a dinner favorite

F W V B Gf Ef

 50 Minutes

 4 People

Ingredients

1 oz. of dried porcini mushrooms
10 oz. of rice (Arborio or Carnaroli)
A pot of boiling water
2 Tbsp. of butter
2 Tbsp. of Evoo
1 organic bouillon cube
½ yellow onion, chopped
3 Tbsp. of grated Parmesan cheese

Directions

Soak the dried mushrooms in 2 cups of warm water for 30 minutes. Drain the mushrooms. Keep the mushroom water: filter it and set it aside.

Peel the onion and chop it finely. Grate the Parmesan cheese and set aside.

Sauté the onion with the oil and half of the butter, on medium heat, until slightly golden. Raise the heat, add the bouillon cube and let it melt – always stirring – then add the mushrooms, ½ cup of hot mushroom water and cook for 20 minutes, covered.

Meanwhile, bring to boil the remaining mushroom water in a small saucepan.

Uncover the mushrooms and let all the remaining liquid evaporate. Add the rice and let it toast – always stirring – for a couple of minutes, until the grains look translucent. This passage is very important because the rice must absorb the fat so that it doesn't absorb too much liquid while cooking and the grains remain separated.

Add 1 cup of the hot mushroom water, stir the rice, and lower the heat to medium-low. When the risotto starts to look too thick, add some hot water, one ladle at a time, stirring often.

It usually takes between 15 and 18 minutes for the rice to cook. Taste it after 12 minutes and, when if feels almost done, adjust for salt if needed, add half a ladle of water, stir, remove from stove and let it sit – covered – for a couple of minutes. Uncover, add the rest of the butter and the Parmesan cheese, stir and serve immediately as it tends to thicken very quickly.

Rice and Green Peas

An Ancient Venetian recipe made for the Doge on St. Mark's day

Sp Gf Ef

 40 Minutes   4 People

Ingredients

12 oz. of shelled green peas
6 oz. of rice (preferably Vialone nano or Arborio)
1 quart of beef stock (homemade or from organic broth cubes)
1 small onion, thinly sliced
2 Tbsp. unsalted butter
2 Tbsp. Evoo
2 Tbsp. lean Pancetta or Prosciutto, in small cubes
1 Tbsp. of parsley, finely minced
1 Tbsp. of fennel leaves, finely minced (optional).
2 Tbsp. Parmesan cheese, grated
Salt
Pepper

Directions

Prepare the stock in advance by boiling a nice piece of beef meat, some beef bones, 1 onion, 1 carrot, and 1 stalk of celery. You can substitute stock with broth made with organic cubes.
Shell the green peas. Melt 1 tbsp. of butter in a sauté pan, add the olive oil, the cubed pancetta (or prosciutto), the parsley, the fennel, and the onion. The fennel is optional, but it makes this rich dish much more digestible. Sauté on medium heat for a few minutes, add the green peas, sauté them with the other ingredients for a couple of minutes, add a ladle of broth and cook for 10 minutes.
Add the rice and keep cooking, stirring often and adding broth, one ladle at a time, so that the rice never gets too dry. The consistency should always be "wavy".
When the rice is cooked (in about 12-15 minutes) add the remaining Tbsp. of butter, the grated Parmesan cheese, and grind some pepper. Stir and serve hot.

Chickpea soup

The utimate winter soup

F W V Gf B

 70 Minutes

 4 People

Ingredients

2 cups of organic dried chickpeas
4 cups of water
3/4 cup long-grain brown rice
1 medium yellow potato
1 stalk of celery
a few sprigs of parsley
1 small sprig of rosemary
1 carrot
2 ripe Roma tomatoes
1 clove of garlic
½ medium yellow onion
4 Tbsp. Evoo
1 tsp. of sea salt
Freshly grated black pepper to taste.

Directions

Soak the chickpeas overnight in a non-metallic vessel.
The following day rinse the chickpeas and transfer them into a pot.
Peel the potato and the carrot and cut them into pieces. Wash the celery and cut it into small sections. Wash the tomatoes and cut them in two.
Peel the garlic, cut it in half, and remove its green core.
Wash the parsley and detach the leaves from the stems.
Peel the onion and add half of it to the other ingredients, cut into sections.
Transfer these ingredients into a pot, add the water and cook for 1 hour, together with the salt and the rosemary.
When the chickpeas are cooked, remove some of them with a slotted spoon and set them apart.
Add the olive oil and blend everything together with an immersion blender until you obtain a silky texture. If too much water has evaporated while cooking, add some water.
Add the chickpeas that you have set apart and the rice. Cook for 20 minutes.
You can add a Tbsp. of Evoo and some freshly ground black pepper to each bowl right before serving.
Serve hot.

Squash soup

Heartwarming, smooth, and sweet

F W V B Gf Ef Df

 50 Minutes

 4 People

Ingredients

1 lb. squash, Kabocha or acorn, peeled and cubed
4 cups of water
1 medium potato, cubed
½ yellow onion, diced
3 tablespoons of extra-virgin olive oil or your favorite oil
1 pinch of nutmeg
Salt (to taste, optional)
4 tsp. of parsley, chopped

Directions

Peel and cube the squash. Kabocha squash has a very hard skin and it's easier to peel it if you first cut it in slices, remove the seeds and peel it with a potato peeler.

Sauté the onion in oil until it turns golden brown. Add the cubed squash, the cubed potato, salt, and a pinch of grated nutmeg. Stir, add the water and cook for 45 minutes, checking that the soup doesn't become too thick. If it does, add more hot water.

Blend with an immersion blender. Right before serving it, sprinkle a teaspoon of chopped parsley on each bowl.

This soup freezes well.

White beans and rice soup

A nutritious, creamy delight

A Gf B Lf Ef V

 50 Minutes

 4 People

Ingredients

6 cups of water
2 cups of dried white beans
1 celery stalk, chopped
1 medium carrot (cubed)
1 medium potato (cubed)
1 leek (chopped, only the white part)
12-15 organic ripe grape tomatoes
2 tablespoons of Evoo
1 small twig of rosemary
1 pinch of baking soda (1/2 teaspoon)
½ cup of rice
2 tsp. Himalayan Salt
Black pepper (to taste, optional)

Directions

Rinse the beans. Soak overnight in cold water with a pinch of baking soda. Sauté the leek, carrot, and celery in Evoo, for 5-7 minutes on medium heat. Add the water, bring to a boil, add the beans, potato, rosemary, the tomatoes cut in half, and the salt. Cook for 35-40 minutes.
Add the rice, stirring once in a while and checking that the soup doesn't become too thick. If that happens, add more boiling water (adding cold water would stop the cooking!). Cook the rice for 12 to 15 minutes and serve the soup warm, with a drizzle of olive oil and grind some black pepper on top.

The eye also wants its share

> "If a man finds himself with bread in both hands, he should exchange one loaf for some flowers of the narcissus, because the loaf feeds the body, but the flowers feed the soul."
> – Muhammad.

As we say in Italy "Anche l'occhio vuole la sua parte", "The eye also wants its share."

The proverb refers to the importance of food presentation because a pleasantly set up dish means care, attention to detail, and love for the food you've cooked.

The way you arrange your vegetables on the plate can make your salad look more inviting; an attentive color combination between your entrée and the side dish it's served with it can enhance the look – and taste – of both of them.

As much as the smell of food can whet your appetite so its presentation can make it more tempting.

Setting a beautiful table creates expectations of dishes as flavorfully pleasant as your setting is aesthetically comely. According to the season, choose your colors as you do with your food: a cold palette of green, yellow and blue hues for the warm season, warm shades of orange, brown, and red for the cold months. To determine what colors look good together, use the color wheel (available online or in craft stores). It will help you to develop a taste for choosing nice combinations.

Depending on the occasion, your table can be formal, elegant, or casual, but make sure you think in advance what impression you want to give your guests on their arrival.

I find flowers particularly welcoming, and I always make a centerpiece for my dinner parties. It can be as simple as a candle surrounded by flowers or greenery, or a sophisticated arrangement for a holiday, or perhaps a whimsical one with herbs and vegetables.

Years ago, I learned that good timing could also play a role in the taste of food.

Some friends of mine kept raving about the fantastic paella that a common acquaintance from Spain made for a dinner party that she hosted every summer. When I was invited the following year, I couldn't wait to find out what made her paella outstanding. When I asked the hostess, she winked at me, saying, "You will see …"

Despite the Spanish fame for tapas, I noticed that very few appetizers were being served while there seemed to be an endless flow of cold and delicious sangria, which kept coming from the kitchen in big pitchers.

In keeping with the Spanish tradition of eating late, dinner was served around nine. By that time, I was famished and a little tipsy from drinking too much sangria, and, looking around, I could tell that the other guests were as well.

The paella was indeed the best I had ever had, but I couldn't tell how much the hunger and inebriation impaired my judgment.

When I complimented the hostess about her paella, she winked at me again and asked, "Did you guess my secret ingredient?"

That evening I learned that a long wait could contribute to making a dish taste even better than it does, but I still prefer my dinners to be enjoyed by my guests without resorting to any tricks.

FISH

Halibut 'en papillotte'   Page   97
Finnish Salmon Pasty   Page   99
Black cod with olives and capers   Page 101
Salmon with orange and mint   Page 103
Halibut with basil pesto   Page 105
Salmon cakes   Page 107
Mediterranean salmon   Page 109

Halibut 'en papillotte'

A refreshing way to prepare white seafood

A B Gf Df Ef

---

 40 Minutes   2 People

Ingredients

2 halibut fillets, about 6 oz. each
16 green olives (like picholine)
3-4 Tbsp. of Evoo
1 tsp. of green pepper berries
Sea salt to taste
A few leaves of basil
A few sprigs of parsley
A few leaves of lemon thyme

Directions

Preheat the oven to 400 F.
Cover a baking pan with a big piece of parchment paper, approx. 3 feet long. You must have enough paper to close it loosely around the halibut.
Remove the pits from the olives.
Grease the center part of the parchment paper with oil and lay the halibut on it. Scatter olives, capers, and herbs on the halibut fillets, and add the remaining oil.
Grind some sea salt on the fish and close the paper loosely around the halibut, but tightly at the seams so that the heat cannot escape while the fish is cooking.
Bake for 20 minutes. Carefully open the paper, starting from the top, to let the steam inside the wrap evaporate for a few seconds before plating.
You can also wrap the fillets individually and place each open wrap directly on the serving plate.

Finnish Salmon Pasty

A delightful Nordic dish

F W

🕐 70 Minutes   👤 4 People

Ingredients

---

160 g. long-grain brown rice
400 ml. water
250 g. smoked salmon (or 350 g. of fresh salmon, steamed or boiled)
1 sheet of puff pastry
150 ml. heavy whipping cream
1 lemon
1 egg
1 Tbsp. of milk
1 tsp. of white pepper

Tip: if you are using smoked salmon, do not add any salt because the fish itself is very salty.

Directions

Combine rice and water in a pot, stir, bring to a full boil, cover with a lid, reduce heat and simmer for 20-25 minutes, until all water gets absorbed.

Wash the lemon, zest the rind, and set aside. While the rice is still warm, add the cream, white pepper, and lemon zest to it, and stir well. Let the rice cool completely.

Preheat the oven to 400F and line a baking sheet with parchment paper.

On a floured surface, roll the puff pastry sheet into a 15" x 15" square. Spread the rice mixture evenly on the puff pastry, leaving a 1-inch edge of pastry all around.

Add the salmon pieces over the rice.

Make the egg wash by cracking the egg into a small bowl, adding the milk, and mixing with a fork.

Brush the empty edge of the pastry with the egg wash. It will help to seal the pastry.

Fold the the pastry edge over the rice/salmon, brush the empty edge of pastry with the egg wash, and carefully shape into a roll. Transfer the roll onto the baking sheet, brush with egg wash and bake for 40-45 minutes, until golden brown.

Let your salmon pasty cool down for a few minutes before cutting it.

Black cod with olives and capers

A revisited Tuscan recipe

A Gf Ef Df

---

 40 Minutes   2 People

Ingredients

4 pieces (as big as a deck of cards) of frozen* or fresh black cod
½ lb. ripe organic halved cherry tomatoes or 7 oz. of tomato sauce
½ yellow onion
2 cloves of garlic
¼ cup of Kalamata olives, pitted and halved
¼ cup of pickled capers
4 Tbsp. of Evoo
a few leaves of basil, shredded by hand, or a tsp. of dried basil
Salt
Pepper

Directions

Peel and finely slice the onion. Peel the garlic, cut it in half and remove its green core. Sauté the onion and the garlic in a pan with Evoo.
Rinse the cod in cold water and pat it dry.
Add the cod to the pan and brown it for a couple of minutes on each side. Turn it with care because it breaks easily.
Add the olives, capers, tomatoes, salt, and pepper, taking into account that the capers and the olives are already salty. Cover with a lid, cook for 10 minutes on medium heat, then uncover, add the basil (shredded or dried) and let evaporate any remaining liquid. Serve warm.

* If you are using frozen cod, the pieces must be bigger than suggested because it loses volume when it thaws. Remember to thaw the fish in the refrigerator overnight before using it.

Salmon with orange and mint

A happy marriage of seafood and citrus

A B Gf Ef Df

_____

 40 Minutes   4 People

Ingredients

A nice fillet of wild salmon, about
2 lbs.
1 whole orange
A few sprigs of mint
4-5 Tbsp. of Evoo
Himalayan salt
2 tsp. of pink peppercorns *

* Pink peppercorns are related to
cashews and can cause an allergic
reaction to those who are allergic to
cashews/tree nuts

Directions

Preheat the oven to 380F.
Wash the mint and pat it dry with a paper towel. Wash the
salmon and pat it dry with paper towels.
Cover an oven pan with a big piece of aluminum foil, approx. 3
feet long.
You must have enough foil to close it loosely around the salmon. Wash the orange and slice it into rounds. Grease the center
part of the aluminum foil with oil, lay the salmon on the foil,
place the orange rounds on top of the salmon fillet, alternating them with the mint sprigs. Add the remaining oil on top
and around the salmon.
Grind some Himalayan salt and add the pink peppercorns.
Close the aluminum foil, loosely around the salmon, but
tightly at the seams so that the heat cannot escape while the
salmon is cooking.
Bake for 20 minutes. Carefully open the aluminum, starting
from the top, to let the steam inside the aluminum wrap
evaporate for a few seconds. Cut the portions and serve, keeping a slice of orange and some mint on top of each slice.
Serve warm.

Halibut with basil pesto

An original and tasty dinner recipe

A B Gf Ef

---

 40 Minutes   2 People

Ingredients

2 halibut fillets, about 5 oz. each
2 medium potatoes
4 Tbsp. basil pesto (see recipe)
3-4 Tbsp. of Evoo
1 Tbsp pine nuts
Himalayan salt

Directions

Preheat the oven to 400 F. Cover a baking pan with a piece of parchment paper, big enough to be closed loosely around the halibut.
Make the basil pesto according to my recipe or, if you have frozen some, thaw it at room temperature. Peel the potatoes and slice them very thinly. Grease the center part of the parchment paper with oil, spread the potatoes on it, each slice slightly overlapping the next one. Grind the Himalayan salt on the potatoes. Lay the halibut fillets on the potatoes, spread the pesto on fish, scatter the pine nuts on it, and drizzle with the remaining oil. Close the paper loosely around the halibut, but tightly at the seams so that the heat cannot escape while the fish is cooking. Bake for 20-25 minutes. Carefully open the paper, starting from the top, to let the steam evaporate for a few seconds.

Salmon cakes

Salmon as finger food

A B Gf

---

 40 Minutes   2 People

Ingredients

---

8 oz. of raw salmon (skin removed)
1 egg
1/2 cup of ground walnuts*
1 stalk of celery
1/2 cup fresh Italian parsley
grated rind of 1/2 lemon
1/4 tsp. salt
Pepper to taste

Caper sauce:

3 Tbsp. homemade mayonnaise (see my recipe)
1 Tbsp. capers
2 tsp. lemon juice
salt to taste
1 Tbsp. chopped fresh parsley
2 Tbsp. Evoo
1 Tbsp. water

Directions

Remove the skin from the salmon and mince the meat with a sharp knife. Chop finely the walnuts, parsley, and celery stalk. Mix all these ingredients with egg, lemon rind, salt, and pepper.
Mix the caper sauce in a small bowl.
Warm up the oven to 380 F. Form the cakes with the salmon mixture. Bake the cakes in an oiled baking dish for 20 minutes. Serve the cakes with the caper sauce.

* If you cannot use nuts, replace them with two Tbsp. of corn flakes crumbs for crunchiness and add 1 Tbsp. of Evoo to prevent the cakes from becoming too dry.

Mediterranean salmon

A complete dinner

A B Gf Df Ef

---

 60 Minutes   6 People

Ingredients

1 big fillet of wild salmon, approx. 2 lb.
3 yellow onions
4 big ripe tomatoes
a few leaves of basil (10-12)
½ cup of Kalamata olives
2 Tbsp. of capers
7 Tbsp. of Evoo
Himalayan salt
Black pepper

Directions

Preheat the oven to 380F.
Wash the basil and pat it dry with a paper towel. Wash the salmon and pat it dry with a paper towel.
Peel the onions and slice them thin. Sauté them in 3 Tbsp. of olive oil in a frying pan until they wilt, continuously stirring, for approx. 10 minutes. They don't need to be completely cooked as they will finish cooking in the oven. Spread evenly the sauté onions on the bottom of an oven pan big enough to contain the salmon.
Wash the tomatoes and slice them into rounds 1/3 inch thick. Lay them over the onions. Grind some salt and some pepper. Place the salmon fillet over the tomatoes, cut the olives in half, and spread them evenly over the salmon. Add the capers, basil leaves, salt, and pepper again, and the remaining olive oil.
Bake for 20-30 minutes at 380 F.
Serve warm.

Of Mushrooms and Marmalade

I'm a firm believer in the old proverb that says that "What goes around, comes around."

It might be a way of the Universe of re-balancing itself or simply the way things work on planet Earth. I've witnessed countless examples where both good and bad actions have found strange ways of ricocheting until they went back to where they had originated, closing an imaginary circle.

Now that we are empty-nesters cooking in large quantities doesn't make any sense for my husband and me. However, I still love the satisfaction that comes from looking at a table covered with food that I have prepared or at a big batch of orange marmalade, wondering what I would do with all that preserve, way too sugary for us to eat often.

The solution is easy: I give my food away. I choose special occasions to plan dinner parties to cook for an army of friends without worrying about overeating because my guests gladly do that.

As for preserves, I've found out that marmalade, jams, and jellies make a very welcome gift. I give a jar to the hostess when I'm invited to dinner; I send a couple of jars to a friend who lives far away; and I bring some to my neighbors, especially the elderly or the single ones.

It's a special little thing that says that you care because you are willing to share what took you a lot of time and labor to make.

That's why my friends and neighbors are always delighted to receive it, mainly because it comes with a perfect deal: I tell them that they can exchange the empty jar with a full one.

I'm pretty sure they think that I'm doing them a favor, while in reality, they are making a big one to me because I love making preserves, and a lot of empty jars are the perfect excuse to keep doing it.

I don't expect anything in return. Materially, that is, because when I see grati-

tude, surprise, and joy in the receivers' eyes, I'm more than satisfied.

However, somehow the balance needs to be re-established and, once in a while, I get surprised with unexpected gifts.

One day I received a phone call from a stranger who said that she had heard from a common acquaintance that I love wild mushrooms, and she happened to have too many chanterelles that she had picked that morning. Would I like to have some?

Of course, I would!

She was at my doorstep ten minutes later, with a beautiful basket of the biggest chanterelles I had ever seen. I told her that I didn't even know they grew in our area, especially in that season.

We chatted for a few minutes, getting to know each other, both of us surprised by how much we had in common. Since she wouldn't accept any money, I went to my cellar and took a jar of my peach/lavender jam and a good bottle of Italian wine, feeling happy that I had some good bartering items at hand.

The same woman came back a few months later. This time she had some freshly picked morels. Did I, by any chance, know how to cook them?

Her timing was perfect. I needed some distraction from a family issue that had been bothering me for a while, and I was home alone, mulling over it.

She refused to come inside because of her muddy boots (she had just come back from the woods where she picked mushrooms), so we stood on my porch, talking until she had to leave. I didn't let her go empty-handed, though. A few days before, I had made my last batch of orange marmalade, having run out of the previous one in a couple of months.

After that second visit, I couldn't stop thinking about these small – but big for me – wonders that happen in my life.

I must say that I'm fortunate because I'm blessed with wonderful friends and neighbors. One gave me a book on antique roses to thank me for the pleasure of walking by my garden and enjoying its beauty or another one who leaves her hens' fresh eggs on my porch just because I let her pick herbs from my garden. Then there's Bill – my gardener – who never forgets to bring me a big bag of vegetables every time he visits his brother, an organic farmer.

I'm grateful to these people not only for their gifts but because I get to feel what others feel when they receive my goodies, even if they are not the same persons to whom I gave my homemade treats. And what marvels me the most is that it always happens at the right time, when I least expect it, but I need it the most.

My story isn't about giving and expecting something in return. It's about the pleasure of giving and the mysterious ways we have to connect by means of mushrooms, marmalade, fresh eggs, books, vegetables, which in the end are symbols of love and kindness.

So please get in the habit of cooking something special and sharing it with friends and neighbors. Make those Christmas cookies even if it's spring and give them away. Bake a cake and give a generous portion of it to your widowed neighbor. And if cooking isn't your specialty, buy a small gift for a friend, even if it's not a special occasion.

One day, when you least expect it but need it, it will come back in the most unexpected form.

MEAT

Chicken Cacciatore   Page 117
Veal with Tuna Sauce   Page 119
Rabbit with Olives   Page 121
Turkey tenderloin with prunes   Page 123
Chicken Tenders with Lemon   Page 125

Chicken Cacciatore

A hearty dinner

A B Gf Df Ef

---

 40 Minutes   2 People

Ingredients

4 organic skinless chicken thighs
1 sweet yellow onion
1 clove of garlic
1 rosemary sprig
20-25 organic cherry tomatoes
4 Tbsp. Evoo
Salt
Pepper

Directions

Peel the onion and cut it into eight slices. Peel the garlic, cut it in half and remove its green core.
Warm up the oil in a pan and sauté the onion and garlic, for 2-3 minutes.
Meanwhile, wash the chicken thighs and pat them dry. Brown the chicken evenly in the pan on medium-high heat for 3-4 minutes on each side, add the rosemary, salt, and pepper.
Cover with a lid and cook for 10 minutes.
Wash the tomatoes, cut them in half, and add them to the chicken. Keep cooking covered, on low heat, until the tomatoes start wilting.
Uncover, let any remaining liquid evaporate, and serve warm.

N.B. Chicken is cooked when its internal temperature is 165F. Poultry meat is very prone to contamination by the dangerous bacterium E. coli. Please remember to wash your hands and every surface that has been in contact with the chicken with hot water and anti-bacterial soap.

Veal with Tuna Sauce

An unexpected and flavorful pairing of surf and turf

Sr V B Gf Ef

 120 Minutes   4 People

Ingredients

1 ½ lb. of veal (round loin or round eye)
5 oz. of canned tuna, oil packed
2 cups of dry white wine
1 egg
1 oz. of pickled capers (plus a few for decoration)
1 small piece of lemon rind
1 carrot
1 stalk of celery
1 medium onion
2-3 cloves
1 bay leaf
1 clove of garlic
1 small bunch of parsley
1 cup of mayonnaise
1 Tbsp. of white vinegar
2-3 anchiovies
Salt
Black peppercorns

Tip: the stock can be filtered, refrigerated and used the following day to make Risotto (see recipe).

Directions

Wash, dry, and tie the meat with a string to keep it together while it's cooking.
Wash the carrot and the celery, and cut them into chunks; peel the onion and cut it in half.
Put the meat and these vegetables in a big pot, together with the peeled garlic clove, clover, bay leaf, lemon peel, a dozen of peppercorns, and the parsley.
Pour the white wine and enough water to cover the meat completely.
Add 2 tsp. of salt and bring to a full boil. Lower the heat and cook on low heat for 50 to 55 minutes, covered with a lid. The meat is cooked when the internal temperature reaches 125 F. Do not overcook otherwise the meat will lose its tenderness.
Remove the meat from the stock and let it cool down on a plate, cover it with a second plate on which you'll put something heavy (like a package of sugar or flour).
Boil the egg and discard the white.
Prepare the tuna sauce.
Put the mayonnaise (see recipe), tuna, capers, anchovies, and the boiled egg yolk in a food processor and blend to obtain a smooth sauce.
Slice the cold meat very thin, arrange the slices on a serving dish and cover them with the tuna sauce.
Cover with foil and refrigerate for 1 hour before serving, so that the meat has time to absorb the flavor from the sauce.
Serve cold.

Rabbit with Olives

An enticing alternative to white meat

A Gf Ef

 70 Minutes

 4 People

Ingredients

A whole rabbit (about 3 lb.)
6 Tbsp. of Evoo
1 Tbsp. of butter
1 yellow onion
3 cloves of garlic
3 sprigs of rosemary
12-15 green olives (unpitted)
12-15 black olives (unpitted)
¾ cup of dry white wine
½ cup of white vinegar
Black pepper
Salt

Directions

Wash the rabbit, cut it into pieces starting from the hind legs.

Fill a big bowl with cold water and the vinegar and soak the pieces of rabbit into it for 5 minutes.

In the meantime, peel the onion and dice it finely. Drain the pieces of rabbit and pat dry with paper towels. Warm up the oil and the butter in a pan and sauté onion and peeled garlic until translucent.

Add the rosemary and brown the pieces of rabbit on both sides. Add the dry white wine, let evaporate for a couple of minutes, add the olives, salt, pepper, lower the heat, and cover with a lid.

Cook on low heat for 50-60 minutes. Should the rabbit look too dry while cooking, add half a ladle of hot water to keep it moist.

Uncover for the last few minutes to let evaporate any remaining moisture and serve warm, perhaps with polenta or potato puree (see my recipes).

Turkey tenderloin with prunes

A successful marriage between sweet and savory

F W Gf Df

🕐 40 Minutes   👤 2 People

Ingredients

1 lb. of organic turkey tenderloin
1 organic Granny Smith apple
10-12 dried prunes
1 sprig of rosemary
2 cloves of garlic
3 Tbsp. of Evoo
1/2 Tbsp. unsalted butter
1 cup of dry white wine
Salt
Black pepper

Directions

Wash the tenderloin; trim any fat, and pat dry with paper towels. On the stove-top, heat the oil and the butter in a pan. Crush the garlic with the back of a spoon without peeling it, and add it to the pan, together with the rosemary.
Brown the meat on all sides for a few minutes, discard the garlic, and add the white wine, let the alcohol evaporate for a couple of minutes on high heat, add salt and pepper, cover with a lid, and cook on low heat for 20 minutes.
Peel the apple, cut it into eight wedges and add it to the pan together with the pitted prunes, and keep cooking for another 10 to 12 minutes. The tenderloins are cooked when the internal temperature – measured with a food thermometer in the thickest part – reaches 165F. Remove the pan from the stove-top, and let it rest for 5 minutes, covered.
Slice the meat and serve warm with some gravy, apples, and prunes.

Chicken Tenders with Lemon

A refreshing way to enjoy chicken

A B Gf

---

 30 Minutes   2 People

Ingredients

---

1 lb. of organic chicken tenders
2 lemons
4 Tbsp. of rice flour
3 Tbsp of olive oil
1 tsp. butter
10- 12 leaves of sage
Salt
White pepper

Directions

Wash the lemons. Grate 1 tsp. of lemon rind and mix it with the rice flour, salt, and white pepper in a shallow dish. Toss the chicken tenders in the flour and coat evenly.
Squeeze the juice of 1 lemon and add 2 Tbsp. of water to it. Cut the other lemon into slices.
Warm up the oil and the butter in a pan.
Transfer the breast tenders and lemon slices to the pan and brown them evenly on both sides. Add the sage leaves, the lemon juice, then cover and cook for 12 to 15 minutes, checking that the chicken doesn't become too dry. If it does, add more warm water until the tenders are well cooked (check with a food thermometer that internal temperature is 165 F).
The rice flour should form a creamy sauce. Adjust for salt and serve warm.

N.B. Please remember to wash your hands and every surface that has been in touch with the chicken with hot water and anti-bacterial soap, since poultry meat is very prone to con-tamination by the dangerous bacterium E. coli.

Shortcuts

We all love shortcuts, especially when they save us time without affecting the quality of the result.

In the kitchen, there are many ways to avoid repetitive and annoying chores. Let me suggest some of them.

If you look at a restaurant kitchen, the cooks have on hand refrigerated drawers full of ready-to-use ingredients, as well as vast and well-stocked pantries and walk-in refrigerators. Indeed, these conveniences must make their job much faster and easier, but we have to find other ways to make our cooking simpler since very few of us can afford such luxuries.

· When a recipe requires a half chopped onion, chop two of them and freeze the extra. Next time you need some chopped onion, it will be ready to use.

· Following the same principle, while you chop some celery and carrot to make a soup, chop more and freeze it. Together with the frozen onion, the base for most of your soups is ready to use in seconds.

· When you make a salad, wash some extra lettuce or mixed greens, dry them in a salad spinner, and transfer them into a Ziploc. It keeps for days in your refrigerator, ready to eat.

· Buy a vacuum sealer. Food lasts much longer when it's vacuum-sealed, allowing you to buy larger quantities, saving yourself some trips to the grocery store for things like cheese, meat, seafood, bread, etc. Use what you need and vacuum-seal the rest of it. Be careful to cut the bag along the sealed line so that you can re-use it. Moreover, whatever you vacuum-seal has no risk of freezer burn.

· Freeze, freeze, freeze! Cook one or two extra portions to use when you are in a rush or don't feel like cooking. As I suggested in its recipe, basil pesto freezes very well. In minutes you'll have the perfect sauce for a quick pasta

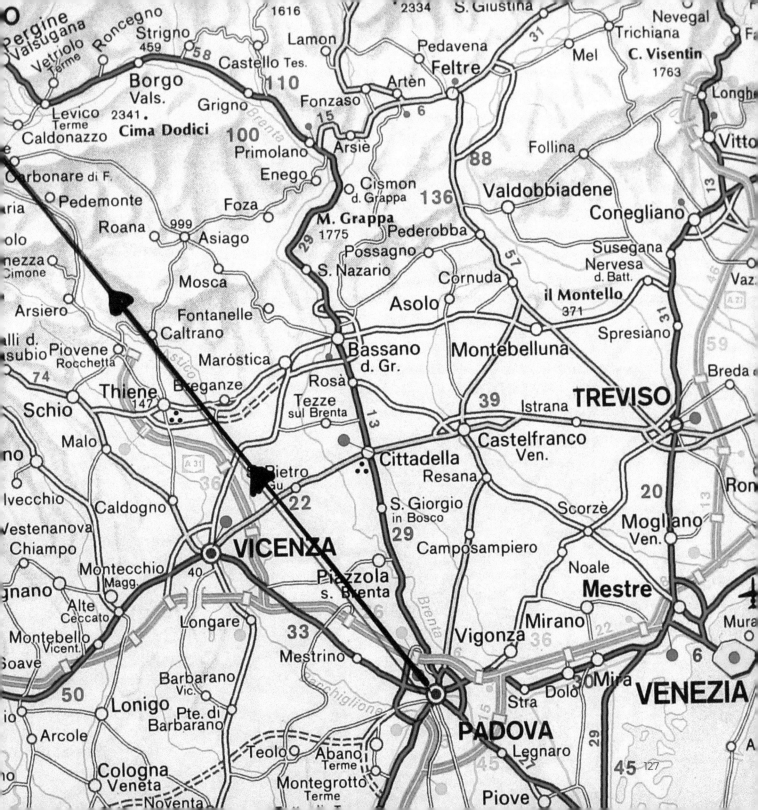

or a tasty dressing for your Caprese salad. Ratatouille freezes well, and so do soups. Thaw them directly in a saucepan (whenever possible, do not use the microwave oven). When you know that you have some food ready to eat in just minutes, you are less tempted to buy and eat processed food with the excuse that you don't have time to cook or you are too hungry to wait.

- If you have a pantry, stock it with the things you use more often, like oil, flour, rice, pasta, coffee, nuts, etc. If you don't have a pantry, re-organize your kitchen to make room for one. It's the perfect opportunity to clean up your cabinets and to throw away any expired food. By moving things around, you'll find the space you need. You can find a great selection of cabinet organizers both online and in stores. With a small investment in time and money, your kitchen will become better organized and easier to work in.

- Plant your herbs. If you don't have a garden, all you need is a pot or two and some potting soil. Herbs are easy to grow and pleasant to see—plant rosemary, cilantro, and thyme in one pot; sage, dill, parsley in another. Mint and oregano have to be planted in separate pots because they grow very fast and tend to suffocate other plants. When the weather gets warm enough, add a plant of basil to your collection of herbs. It's such a satisfaction to snap a sprig of rosemary or a few leaves of sage for your recipes! They are right there, only a few steps away in your garden, on your balcony, or your porch, and, most importantly, they haven't lost most of their fragrance by sitting for days in a supermarket refrigerator. Just remember to water them. Although most herbs are drought-tolerant (for example, sage, rosemary, oregano), others (like basil and parsley) need to drink often to stay alive.

I hope to have inspired some changes that will make your cooking life easier.

DESSERTS

Orange Ring Cake   Page 133

Holiday Cream   Page 135

Avocado Parfait   Page 137

Meringata   Page 139

Fruit Salad   Page 141

Apple Strudel   Page 144

Peach Tiramisù   Page 147

Poached Pears   Page 149

Apple Cream Torte   Page 151

Cornmeal cookies   Page 153

Cantucci   Page 155

Zaeti   Page 157

Hazelnut Amaretti   Page 159

Zabaione   Page 161

Hazelnut Cake   Page 163

Orange Ring Cake

A delightful winter dessert

W V Df

---

 60 Minutes   8 People

Ingredients

4 organic eggs
150 g. of organic sugar
2 organic oranges
350 g. of pastry flour
150 g. of rice oil
15 g. of baking powder
8 g. of orange extract
1 Tbsp. of powdered sugar
1 pinch of salt

Directions

Preheat oven to 360F with rack on lower middle position.
Grease a ring or Bundt cake pan and set aside.
Sift together the flour and the baking powder.
Wash the oranges, grate their rind first and then squeeze their juice. Set aside.
Break the eggs into a large bowl, add a pinch of salt and start beating with a hand electric mixer.
Add the sugar a little at a time and keep beating until pale and fluffy.
Still beating on medium speed, add the orange juice, the orange rind, the rice oil, and the orange extract. When these ingredients are well blended together, start adding the flour with the baking powder, a little at a time, until you get a smooth batter.
Pour the batter into the greased ring or Bundt cake pan and smooth the top evenly.
Bake for 35-40 minutes. Let cake cool before removing it from the pan.
Dust the cake with powdered sugar right before serving it.

Holiday Cream

A heavenly light custard

A V Gf

 60 Minutes   8 People

Ingredients

4 organic egg yolks
4 Tbsp. sugar
2 Tbsp. of corn starch
4 cups of organic 2% milk
a few drops of real vanilla extract
2 cups (1 pint) of organic heavy
whipping cream
the grated rind of 1 organic lemon

Directions

Beat the egg yolks and sugar until pale and fluffy.
Meanwhile, bring the milk to a boil in a saucepan. Remove it from heat and add the vanilla.
Wash the lemon and grate its rind; add it to beaten egg yolks.
A little at a time, incorporate the corn starch into the beaten egg yolks, stirring.
Transfer this mixture into a non-stick saucepan, add half a cup of hot milk, whisking with a hand whisk to avoid forming lumps. Put the saucepan on low heat, add the remaining milk a little at a time to avoid cooking the egg mixture and bring it to a boil, always stirring.
Cook for three to four minutes. The result must be a smooth sauce. Should any lumps form, you can strain the cream through a fine mesh colander or blend it with an immersion blender. Cool down the cream in an ice bath and refrigerate for at least three hours, covered with a plastic film in direct contact with the surface. You can prepare this base for your cream one or two days in advance, as long as you keep it refrigerated in an air-tight container.
Right before serving, whip the whipping cream with an electric beater and fold it into the egg cream with a spatula. Serve cold.

Avocado Parfait

A surprisingly delicious way to enjoy avocados

A B V Gf Ef

 30 Minutes

 4 People

Ingredients

2 ripe avocados
1 organic navel orange
1 pinch of cinnamon
4 tsp. of agave syrup
8 Tbsp. of gluten-free rolled oats
4 Tbsp. of unsweetened coconut cream
1 small piece of butter
4 tsp. of organic brown sugar

Directions

Melt the butter in a non-stick frying pan, add the sugar, the gluten-free oats and toast this mix until golden brown, stirring constantly, about 7 to 10 minutes.
Divide half of this toasted mix among 4 small serving glasses and set aside the rest.
Grate half the rind of the orange into a mixing bowl and add the juice of half orange.
Cut the avocados in half, discard the pit and mash the pulp with a fork.
Stir it together with the cinnamon, the agave syrup, the coconut cream, the orange rind and the juice until you obtain a smooth cream. Layer the cream on top of the toasted oats in the serving glasses, top with the remaining toasted oats and refrigerate for no longer than two hours before serving, otherwise the crunchy oats will become soggy.

Meringata

A dessert from Heaven

A V Gf

---

 3 Hours + Freezing time

 8 People

Ingredients

---

6 egg whites
180 g. superfine sugar
180 g. powdered sugar
1 pinch of cream of tartar
400 g. heavy whipping cream
60 g. powdered sugar

Directions

Preheat the oven to 240 F.
Bring the eggs at room temperature. In the meantime, cover a baking sheet with parchment paper and draw on it two circles of the same internal circumference of your spring pan.
Separate the whites from the yolks making sure there is no trace of yolk in the whites.
Add the cream of tartar to the whites and start beating – either with a standing mixer or with a hand beater – gradually increasing the speed.

When you reach high speed, start adding the superfine sugar, a little at a time. When the egg whites have become very stiff, start adding the powdered sugar, a little at a time.
Put the meringue mix into a pastry bag and make two discs by filling in the circles on the parchment paper, starting from the center and without leaving any gaps.
The meringue circles should be 3/4 to 1-inch high.
Use the remaining meringue mix in the pastry bag to make small meringues that you will use later to decorate your cake.
Lower the oven temperature to 200 F and bake for 2 hours, checking regularly that your meringues doesn't start to brown. Meringues should not cook but simply dry out.
For the last 30 minutes of baking, keep the oven door slightly open using a ball of aluminum foil.
Turn off the oven, open the door completely and let the meringue cool down, preferably overnight.
When you are ready to assemble the cake, whip the cream, adding the powdered sugar a little at a time.
Put the first disc of meringue on the bottom of a spring pan and cover it with 1/3 of the whipped cream. Cover with the second disc of meringue, another 1/3 of whipped cream, and set aside the remaining cream. Freeze for 3 – 4 hours.
30 to 40 minutes before serving the meringata, remove it from the spring pan, cover its surface and sides with the remaining whipped cream, crush the extra meringues, and use them to decorate your dessert.

Fruit Salad

A refreshing dessert

W F V B Gf Df Ef

---

 30 Minutes   4 People

Ingredients

2 pears
1 apple
2 bananas
3 cups of mixed frozen berries
½ cup of diced dried papaya
½ cup of raisins
a handful of pine nuts
1/3 cup of walnuts pieces
1 orange, juiced
1 lemon, juiced
2 Tbsp. brown organic sugar
½ cup of sparkling water
1 bay leaf

Directions

Soak the raisins in warm water. Thaw the frozen berries at room temperature. Squeeze the orange and the lemon, pour their juice into a bowl big enough to contain all the ingredients, add the sugar, the sparkling water, the bay leaf, and stir. As you cut the fruit, add it to this juice. Wash the pears and apples, peel them, and dice them. Peel the bananas, cut in half lengthwise and slice them ¼ inch thick. Drain the raisins and add them to the bowl, together with the remaining ingredients. Toss, refrigerate, and remove the bay leaf before serving.

A Secret Recipe

On a snowy winter day, I found a silver lining in the gray clouds: to bake an apple strudel. I adore this dessert, and I have found a way to make it gluten-free, so I'll make a variation of the recipe that Frau Waltraud gave me many years ago during a vacation in the beautiful Pusterthal, a valley in the Italian Alps.

I had made a strudel before, following my mother's recipe. Still, its filling lacked that particular texture that is a delicate combination between the softness of the cooked apples and the brittleness of the rest of the stuffing.

One summer night at her hotel in Toblach, Frau Waltraud – a stern widow in her sixties, always picture-perfectly dressed in the traditional costume of South Tyrol – delighted her guests with a feast of different kinds of strudel: peach strudel, cherry strudel, apricot strudel, blueberry strudel, and the classic apple strudel.

The following day I tried to get the recipe from Frau Waltraud, but she answered with such a firm "Nein!" – I must explain that in that part of Northern Italy, the first language is German because it used to be part of Austria – that I didn't dare to insist. A few days later, though, I saw her casting the stitches for a knitting project, and I asked her if she wanted me to show her an easier way to do it. My technique turned out to be so much easier than hers that she decided to surrender the secret of her unforgettable dessert. Since austere people often feel uncomfortable with their kindness, Frau Waltraud casually put a folded piece of paper in my hand with the apple strudel recipe. She warned me that I would never equal her strudel anyway because what made the crust so smooth and delicate was the butter from a particular farm nearby.

She was right: my strudel is but a faint resemblance of hers, but I'm still so satisfied with my modest result that I think it's worth passing on this strudel recipe.

Apple Strudel

The quintessential Tyrolean dessert

V B GF Ef

---

 90 Minutes   6 People

Ingredients

4 organic apples, preferably golden delicious

1 sheet of gluten-free puff pastry

½ cup golden raisins, soaked in water

1 tsp. of ground cinnamon

1 Tbsp. butter + more for greasing

1 Tbsp. organic sugar

½ cup almonds, ground

½ cup of gluten-free bread crumbs

1 Tbsp. confectioner sugar for dusting

1 cup of heavy cream, whipped.

Directions

Preheat the oven to 380 F.

Soak the raisins in a small bowl filled with warm water.

Peel and core the apples, and cut them into small cubes. Soak them in a bowl filled with water and lemon juice, so that they won't discolor.

Grind the almonds, not too small. Melt 1 Tbsp. of butter in a non-stick frying pan, add the sugar, the ground almonds, and the bread crumbs. Toast this mix until golden brown, stirring constantly, about 7 to 10 minutes.

Transfer this toasted mix into a bowl, add the drained apples, the drained raisins, the cinnamon, and toss well.

With a rolling pin, roll the dough as evenly as possible, trying to make a rectangle about 20" by 14". Transfer the dough onto a big towel dusted with gluten-free flour. The towel will help you roll the strudel without breaking it. Spread the filling on the dough, leaving a border of uncovered dough – about 2 inches wide – all around the filling.

Fold the shorter border over the filling first. With a small brush, wet this folded border with water. This way, when you roll the strudel, the wet dough will adhere to the rest of the dough, preventing the filling from spilling out.

Form the strudel by raising the longer side of the towel and pushing with your hands, until you obtain a roll. With the brush, wet the inside of the last border of dough to seal the strudel. Flatten the top with your hands.

Grease a baking pan with some butter and dust it with gluten-free flour. Carefully transfer the strudel to the baking pan.

Cook at 380 F for 15 minutes, then lower the temperature to 360 F and cook for 45 more minutes or until golden/brown.

While the strudel is cooking, whip the heavy cream and keep it in the fridge until ready to serve the dessert.

Let the strudel cool down, dust with the confectioner sugar, and serve at room temperature with a dollop of whipped cream.

Peach Tiramisù

A delicious variation of a classic dessert

S Ef

---

 30 Minutes   4-6 People

Ingredients

---

4 ripe yellow peaches (about 2 lbs.)
4 Tbsp. Turbinado cane sugar
7 oz. mascarpone cheese
7 oz. Amaretto cookies
30-34 lady finger cookies
1 ½ cup of milk
2 Tbsp. unsweetened cocoa powder
4 Tbsp. rum

Directions

Wash, peel, and cut the peaches into chunks. Cook them in a pan with the sugar for about 15 minutes, stirring often. Let the peaches cool down and blend them into a smooth cream with an immersion blender.

Add the mascarpone to the peaches, one tablespoon at a time, whipping well to avoid forming lumps. Put the milk and rum in a shallow dish and quickly soak the ladyfingers one at a time. The cookies shouldn't get soggy. Make the first layer of ladyfingers in a deep serving dish and spread evenly half of the peach/mascarpone cream over them.

Finely crush the amaretto cookies by putting them in a plastic bag and pressing them with a rolling pin. Scatter half of them over the cream.

Make the second layer of soaked ladyfingers but this time layer them perpendicularly to the first layer. Think north-south for the first layer and east-west for the second. This way the portions won't fall apart when you serve your dessert. Spread the remaining cream and scatter the rest of the cookie crumbs.

Cover with plastic film and refrigerate for at least 3 hours. Before serving, dust the cocoa powder on top.

Poached Pears

For a light meal end

F W V B Gf

---

 40 Minutes   4 People

Ingredients

4 organic Bosc pears
1 cup of red wine
½ cup organic sugar
½ cup of water
1 pinch of cinnamon
5 or 6 cloves
2 oz. of dark chocolate

Directions

Wash the pears and peel them. Choose a saucepan tall enough for the pears to cook standing up. Warm up the water and wine, add the sugar, cinnamon, and cloves, and bring to a boil, stirring to dissolve the sugar. Lower the heat, add the pears, and cook uncovered for 10 minutes. This way the alcohol in the wine will evaporate. Cover and cook for 20 more minutes.
The pears are ready when they are still firm but not mushy, so after 15 minutes test them at the bottom with a fork.
If the liquid in which the pears have been cooked is not thick enough, remove the pears and let boil – uncovered – until it becomes like syrup.
Serve warm or cold, pouring some cooking syrup over the pears and grating some dark chocolate on them.

Apple Cream Torte

Love at first bite

A V B

---

 90 Minutes   8 People

Ingredients

1 ½ lb. organic apples (such as Gala, Fuji, Cameo)
3 large organic eggs at room temperature
1 cup all-purpose flour
1 cup organic sugar
3/4 cup heavy whipping cream
1 lemon
1 tsp. vanilla extract
1 ½ tsp. phosphate-free baking powder
1 pinch of salt
Powdered sugar for dusting
Crème fraîche for serving (optional)

Directions

Preheat the oven to 330 F. Grease a 9-inch spring-form pan, dust it with some flour, and set aside.
Peel the apples and cut them into slices. Put them in a bowl filled with water and lemon juice, to avoid discoloration.
In a small bowl, mix the flour, salt, and baking powder.
In a large mixing bowl, beat the eggs and the sugar at high speed until thick and fluffy. Reduce speed, add cream and vanilla, and beat for another minute. Reduce speed further and blend in flour, baking powder and salt.
Drain the apples and pat them dry with paper towel.
Gently fold the apples into the mixture, using a spatula and making sure to coat them evenly with the batter.
Pour the batter into the spring-form pan and even the top with the spatula. Bake for 60–75 minutes, until the top is golden/brown and a toothpick inserted in the dough comes out clean. Let the cake cool on a rake, then run a knife between the cake and the pan rim. Remove pan rim and cool the cake at least 10 minutes longer. Dust with powdered sugar and serve with a dollop of crème fraîche (optional).

Recipe from Sunset Magazine – September 2016

Cornmeal cookies

An old family recipe from Piedmont

F W V Gf B

---

 45 Minutes   120 Cookies

Ingredients

1 cup of organic corn meal
1 cup of organic gluten-free flour
Half cup of organic sugar
Grated rind of 1 organic lemon
1 pinch of salt
3 oz. of unsalted butter at room temperature
2 whole organic eggs
2 tsp. of baking powder

Directions

Mix all the ingredients in a bowl and knead with your hands to obtain smooth dough. On a floured surface, roll small portions of the dough into "snakes". Cut snakes into half-inch pieces, and lay them onto parchment paper on a cookie sheet.
Lightly press a fork on their surface to form grooves.
Bake at 350F for 12 minutes.

Tip: Make one batch with yellow corn flour and one with blue corn flour.

Cantucci

A classic and delightful biscuit from Tuscany

🕐 45 Minutes   👤 50 Cookies

Ingredients

270 g. (9.5 oz.) baking flour
150 g. (5 oz.) sugar
2 eggs + 1 yolk for brushing
1 oz. of butter at room temperature
4 g. (1 tsp.) baking powder
100 g. (3 oz.) organic almonds, whole,
unpeeled, unroasted
Grated rind of 1/2 organic orange
1 pinch of salt
1 Tbsp. heavy whipping cream
10 g. (0.3 oz.) sweet Marsala wine

Tip: Cantucci make a great dessert
paired with a glass of Port wine.

Directions

Preheat the oven to 400 F.
In a bowl, mix the 2 eggs, salt, and sugar, just enough to melt the sugar, stirring but not whipping. In another bowl mix the flour and the baking powder, then add them to the egg/sugar mix. Add the marsala wine, the grated orange peel, cream, and butter cut into small pieces. Knead with your hands to obtain smooth dough. Add the almonds to the dough and knead until they are evenly distributed.
Divide the dough into 2 pieces and roll one at a time into a long cylinder approx. 1 inch in diameter. Place the two cylinders onto on a cookie sheet covered with parchment paper. Brush with egg yolk. The cylinders will flatten while baking. Bake at 400 F for about 18-20 minutes or until they have a slight golden color.
Let them cool down for 10-12 minutes, and in the meantime lower the oven temperature to 320 F. Then cut the cylinders at an angle into ½ inch slices using a sharp serrated knife. Place back these slices onto the baking sheet covered with parchment paper and return to the oven for 16-18 minutes.
As the cantucci cool down, they will dry and taste better (if you can resist the temptation).

Zaeti

The small yellow cookies, an ancient recipe from Venice

F W V Gf

---

 45 Minutes   40 Cookies

Ingredients

---

300 g. (10.6 oz.) of organic corn flour + 1 tablespoon for tossing the raisins
100 g. (3.5 oz.) of organic gluten-free baking flour
140 g. (5 oz.) of organic sugar
140 g. (5oz.) of raisins
150 g. (5.3 oz). of unsalted butter at room temperature
3 egg yolks
50 g. (2 oz.) of Grappa liqueur
100 g. (3.5 oz.) of warm water
Grated rind of 1/2 organic lemon
8 g. (1 tsp.) of baking powder
1 pinch of salt
1 Tbsp. of heavy whipping cream (optional)

Tip: You can substitute the gluten-free flour with all-purpose flour.

Directions

Mix the warm water and Grappa and let the raisins soak while you mix the other ingredients. Mix all the dry ingredients in a bowl (the two flours, sugar, baking powder and salt), add the butter cut into small pieces and the 3 egg yolks. Knead with your hands to obtain smooth dough. Drain the raisins and toss them in the extra Tbsp. of flour. Transfer them into a colander and shake off the flour in excess. Add the raisins and the grated lemon rind to the dough and knead.
If the dough tends to fall apart, add 1 Tbsp. of heavy whipping cream. Wrap the dough in plastic and refrigerate for 30 minutes.
Divide the dough into 3 pieces and roll one at a time into a cylinder approx. 1 inch in diameter. Cut the cylinder into ½ inch slices and lay them onto on a cookie sheet covered with parchment paper.
Bake at 360 F for about 15 minutes or until they have a nice golden color.
Let the Zaeti cool down and dry for a couple of hours, then dust them with powdered sugar.

Hazelnut Amaretti

Delightful cookies that melt in your mouth

F W V

 45 Minutes   40 Cookies

Ingredients

2 cups all purpose flour
1 cup organic sugar
14 Tbsp (or 7 oz.) unsalted butter (like Kerrygold Irish butter)
2 cups hazelnut flour *
3 tsp. baking powder

* If you cannot find hazelnut flour, you can finely grind dry roasted, unsalted hazelnuts.

Directions

Preheat oven to 340 F and line two large baking sheets with parchment paper. Melt the butter. In a large mixing bowl, combine all the ingredients to obtain a smooth dough. Take small amounts of dough and shape them into small balls (1/2 inch in diameter) with your fingertips.
Transfer onto the parchment-lined baking sheets, leaving 1/2 inch between each line and each row to give the amaretti space to rise as they cook. Bake for 18 to 20 minutes or until golden brown. Let cool at room temperature and enjoy.

Zabaione

An unforgettable delight for the palate

A V Gf Df

 20 Minutes   4 People

Ingredients

4 egg yolks
4 Tbsp. superfine sugar
1/3 cup Moscato wine

Directions

Using a heat-proof bowl, beat the egg yolks and sugar until pale and fluffy.

Place the bowl over a pot of simmering water, making sure that the bottom doesn't touch the water. Cook over low heat, adding the Moscato wine a little at a time, whisking constantly with a hand whisk to incorporate air, with a delicate up-and-down movement. Zabaione should never boil, as it may cause eggs to curdle.

When the mixture starts to get fluffy and thick, remove from heat and serve in cups, with dark chocolate curls or some nutmeg on top.

Tip: adding a teaspoon of corn starch prevents the zabaione from deflating while cooking.

Hazelnut Cake

An Italian family recipe from Piedmont

A V Gf

---

 60 Minutes   8 People

Ingredients

---

8 oz. of hazelnuts
3 Tbsp. of organic brown sugar
2 Tbsp. corn starch
2 eggs + 1 egg white
4 Tbsp. butter, melted
½ cup of water
2 tsp. baking powder
1 pinch of salt

Directions

Preheat the oven to 360 F.
Grind the hazelnuts together with the sugar to obtain a floury meal.
In a mixing bowl, mix the hazelnut meal, the corn starch, the baking powder, and the salt. Add the 2 eggs, the melted butter, and the water, stirring well.
In a separate bowl, whip the egg white with an electric beater until white and stiff. Add the whipped egg white to the mix by folding it in with a spatula, with delicate movements from the bottom to the top.
Grease a round 10-inch baking pan and pour the mix into it.
Cook for 25/30 minutes at 360 F. Remove from baking pan, let cool on a cooling rack, and serve at room temperature.
Hazelnut cake is usually served with Zabaione (see recipe).

SAUCES

Tomato Sauce   Page 167

Green Sauce   Page 168

Bolognese Ragù   Page 169

Basil Pesto   Page 170

Celery and Macadamia Pesto   Page 171

Mayonnaise   Page 172

Bechamel   Page 173

Tomato Sauce

The easiest and healthiest tomato sauce

Sr V B Gf Ef Df

---

 120 Minutes   Yelds eight 1-pint jars

Ingredients

---

8 lb. ripe, organic tomatoes (preferably
Roma or San Marzano)
Basil, approx. 20 leaves
Parsley, handful of leaves
1 small onion
2 cloves of garlic (optional)

Directions

Wash the tomatoes and cut them in half. Peel the onion and cut it
into quarters. Peel the garlic. Wash the basil and the parsley.
Put the tomatoes and the onion in a big pot, together with the
garlic, the parsley, and 10 leaves of basil. Reserve the other leaves for
the canning jars. Bring to a full boil, lower the heat and let cook for
30 minutes.
Strain the tomatoes with a hand food mill. Return to the pot and let
the resulting sauce boil uncovered for another 30-40 minutes, stirring every few minutes so that the sauce doesn't stick to the bottom
of the pot. Remove any foam that floats to the surface.
The result must be a sauce not too thick and not too runny.
To can the tomato sauce, transfer it into clean canning jars when it's
still hot, leaving 1/2 inch space between the sauce and the rim of the
can. Put a basil leaf on the sauce, close immediately each jar with
its lid. I put a clean cotton rag on the bottom of a big pot to avoid
the rattling noise of the glass jars during the sterilization process.
Arrange the jars on the rag, keeping them upright. Fill the pot with
hot water, making sure there is at least ½ inch of water covering the
lids. I cover the pot with its lid and let boil for 40 to 60 minutes. It's
very important that you let the jars cool in the pot before removing
them.
The sterilized tomato sauce jars last for one year if unopened. Once
you open a jar, though, you should keep it in the refrigerator for
max. 3 days, or in the freezer until you need to use it again. Once
thawed, you cannot freeze it again.

Green Sauce

Perfect with meat

F W V Df Ef

🕐 20 Minutes   👤 4 People

Ingredients

---

6 Tbsp. of minced parsley
1 clove of garlic
1 oz. of bread
2 Tbsp. of tomato sauce (see recipe)
3 Tbsp. of red wine vinegar
3 anchovies
1 pinch of salt

Directions

Remove the parsley leaves from the stems and wash them.
In a small bowl, soak the bread crumb in vinegar.
Chop together parsley, garlic, and anchovies in a small food processor. Transfer into a small mixing bowl.
Put the soaked bread in a mesh strainer and squeeze out the vinegar. Add it to the other ingredients in the bowl, together with the tomato sauce. Stir well.
Serve with white or red meats.

Bolognese Ragù

A classic pasta condiment

A Gf Ef

_____

 120 Minutes   4 People

Ingredients

———

1 lb. of mixed ground meat (veal, pork, and beef)
1 carrot
1 stalk of celery
half yellow onion
2 cloves of garlic
1 sprig of rosemary
1 cup of hot water
¼ cup of olive oil
1 cup of tomato sauce (see my recipe)
1 cup of milk

Directions

———

Chop finely the onion, the carrot, the celery, and sauté in olive oil until golden, together with the garlic.
Add the rosemary, and the meat, then brown the meat for 5 minutes on high heat. Add salt and pepper, then cover and simmer for 60-90 minutes. If the sauce gets too dry, add some hot water.
Uncover, add the hot milk and let it evaporate for 5 minutes, stirring often. The milk will balance the acidity of the tomato sauce.

Basil Pesto

A delightful sauce from the Italian Riviera

Sr V Gf B Ef

---

 20 Minutes   4 People

Ingredients

———

1 bunch of fresh basil
2 Tbsp. of pine nuts
4-5 Tbsp. of Evoo
1/2 oz. of pecorino cheese
1/2 oz. Parmesan cheese
Salt

Directions

———

Wash the basil and remove the leaves from the stems. There should be at least fifty leaves. Combine all ingredients in the blender, olive oil first. Start on low and slowly increase the speed. If the ingredients don't blend well, add more olive oil or one tablespoon of water. The result should be a smooth, light-green sauce, with small pieces of its ingredients.

Celery and Macadamia Pesto

An exceptional sauce for your pasta

A V B Ef Gf

 20 Minutes   4 People

Ingredients

1 oz. of fresh celery leaves
1 oz. of spinach leaves
1 oz. of macadamia nuts
1 oz. pecorino cheese
6 Tbsp. of Evoo

Directions

Wash the celery leaves and the spinach. Put the first four ingredients in the blender with 2 Tbsp. of Evoo. Blend on low and slowly increase the speed. Add 2 more Tbsp. of Evoo and blend for a few more seconds. If the ingredients don't blend well, add one tablespoon of water. Taste and adjust for salt. The result should be a smooth, light-green sauce.

Mayonnaise

Essential for many recipes

A V Gf Df

---

 20 Minutes   4 People

Ingredients

———

1 egg at room temperature
a few drops of lemon juice
1 cup of olive oil
a pinch of salt

Directions

———

Break the egg in the plastic beaker of your hand blender or in any a tall container with a small base. The egg must be at room temperature. If you forgot to take it out of the fridge in advance, put it in a cup of warm water for 15 minutes.
Add ¾ cup of olive oil (not extra-virgin because the flavor of the mayonnaise will be too strong), a pinch of salt, and beat for a few seconds with the hand blender at high speed. Add a few drops of lemon juice and the remaining oil, and blend for a few more seconds. Taste and adjust for salt or lemon.

Bechamel

A French mother sauce

A V Ef

_____

🕐 30 Minutes　　👤 4 People

Ingredients

————

4 Tbsp. unsalted butter
3 Tbsp. all-purpose flour
2 cups 2% milk
Salt
Pepper
A pinch of nutmeg

Directions

————

Warm up the milk in a saucepan.
Melt the butter in another saucepan. Add the flour a table-spoon at a time, constantly stirring, and cook for a few minutes, making sure that mixture remains a nice yellow color and doesn't turn brown.
Add the hot milk a little at a time, stirring fast to avoid forming any lumps.
Add salt and pepper, the nutmeg, and cook for 20 minutes, always stirring.
The result should be a velvety white sauce, not too runny and not too thick.

SIDE DISHES

Ratatouille   Page 177
Celery root coleslaw   Page 178
Pickled onions   Page 179
Roasted bell peppers   Page 180
Black rice with lemon   Page 181
Sautéd Mushrooms   Page 182
Fennel au gratin   Page 183

Ratatouille

A Mediterranean dish

Sr B V Gf Ef Df

---

 60 Minutes   6 People

Ingredients

---

1 yellow onion
1 yellow bell pepper
1 red bell pepper
1 green bell pepper
1 eggplant
2 zucchini
6 tomatoes, preferably San Marzano or Roma
2 cloves of garlic, cut in half
6 Tbsp. of Evoo
10 leaves of basil
Salt and Pepper

Directions

Wash and dry all the vegetables.

Since the different vegetables have different cooking times, they must be added at the right time otherwise some will overcook while others will under-cook.

Remove all the seeds and the white internal skin of the bell peppers. Cut them into 1-inch squares. Peel the onion, cut it in half, then cut each half into eight sections.

Peel the garlic, cut it in half and remove its green core.

Warm up the Evoo in a big frying pan. Add the onion and garlic to the pan, sauté them until they start to turn golden, stirring often.

Add the bell peppers and sauté them – stirring often – for 10 minutes.

Add pepper and salt and cook, covered and at low temperature, for at least 15 minutes.

Meanwhile, cut the eggplant into 1-inch squares, removing the central part with the seeds, and add it to the bell peppers.

Wash the tomatoes and slice them into four sections. Add them to the pan and cook for 10 minutes.

Cut the zucchini into ½ inch rounds and add them to the ratatouille. Finally, wash the basil leaves and add them too.

Cook – covered – until all the ingredients start to blend together. Should the ratatouille look too dry while it's cooking, add some hot water. If, on the contrary, it looks too watery when all the ingredients are almost done, cook uncovered on high heat for the last five minutes. Serve warm or cold.

Celery root coleslaw

A healthy variation to the traditional recipe

A V B Df Gf

---

 20 Minutes   4 People

Ingredients

1 celery root
3 Tbsp. of mayonnaise (see recipe)
Salt
Pepper

Directions

Make the mayonnaise following my recipe.
Peel the celery root with a potato peeler and julienne very thinly.
Add the mayonnaise, adjust for salt, grind some pepper to taste, toss and serve.

Pickled onions

A complement to many dishes, from salads to cheese, from meats to seafood.

A V Gf Ef Df

_____

 10 Minutes   4 People

Ingredients

———

1 big red onion
½ cup champagne vinegar or white vinegar
2 Tbsp. Evoo
Salt to taste

Directions

———

Peel the onion and slice it thinly. Sauté the onion with the olive oil in a pan and, when it starts to become translucent, add the vinegar. Keep cooking on medium/high heat until most of the vinegar has evaporated.

Roasted bell peppers

A summer favorite

Sr V B Gf Ef Df

---

 60 Minutes   4 People

Ingredients

————

4 bell organic peppers, of different colors
4 Tbsp. of Evoo
1 clove of garlic
1 Tbsp. of minced parsley
1 pinch of salt

Directions

————

Preheat the oven to 400 F.
Wash and dry the bell peppers. Grease your hands with the Evoo and spread it evenly on the bell peppers. Line a baking pan with parchment paper, place the oiled bell peppers on it and cook in the oven, for about 40 minutes, carefully turning them on all sides to roast them evenly. Let the bell peppers cool down, then peel them. The external skin should come off very easily once the peppers are cold, otherwise wait longer. Remove all the seeds and cut the peppers into quarters. Wash and mince the parsley. Peel the garlic, remove its green core and slice it thinly. Transfer the bell peppers onto a serving plate, dress with olive oil, garlic, parsley, and salt.

Black rice with lemon

A quick side dish to pair with your meat and fish entrees

A V B Gf Ef

 40 Minutes   4 People

Ingredients

1 cup of black rice
1 ¾ cups of water
1 Tbsp. butter
1 lemon
1 tsp. salt

Directions

Combine the rice, water, and salt in a pot, and bring to a boil. Then cover, reduce heat and simmer for 30 minutes. Remove from heat and let sit for a few minutes.
Cut the butter into small pieces in a serving bowl, then add the cooked rice.
Wash and dry the lemon and grate the lemon rind on the rice, toss well and serve warm.

Sautéd Mushrooms

A tasty side dish for the cold season

A V B Gf Df Ef

 30 Minutes   4 People

Ingredients

1 lb. of mixed mushrooms, like Portobello, Shiitake, Maitake, Oyster, Beech, etc.
4 Tbsp. of Evoo
1 clove of garlic, minced
2 Tbsp. of minced parsley
1 tsp. of salt

Directions

Clean the mushrooms very carefully, discarding the hard part of the stems, but don't wash them. Cut them into small pieces. Peel the garlic and mince it very small. Wash the parsley and mince the leaves.
Warm up the Evoo in a pan, add parsley and garlic and sauté for a few minutes, but don't let the garlic turn brown. Add the mushrooms, sauté them stirring often, then add the salt. The salt will help them release enough water to complete the cooking. Cover with lid and cook for 15-20 minutes at low heat. Serve warm.

Fennel au gratin

A low-calorie side dish

A V Gf Ef

_____

 30 Minutes   2 People

Ingredients

2 fennel bulbs
3 Tbsp. Evoo
2 Tbsp. of grated Parmesan cheese
Salt to taste

Directions

Discard the green part of the fennel bulbs, wash them, and cut them into eights, starting from where you cut off the green part.
Steam or boil the fennel, about 12-15 minutes. Drain, transfer into a non-stick oven dish, add the olive oil and salt, toss and sprinkle the grated Parmesan cheese on top.
Broil in the oven until golden-brown, about 5 to 7 minutes.
Serve warm.

Abbreviations & Conversions

Abbreviations

B = biological
Df = dairy free
Ef = egg free
Gf = gluten free
V = vegetarian

Sp = spring recipe
Sr = summer recipe
F = fall recipe
W = Winter recipe
A = All-season recipe

Tbsp. = Tablespoon
tsp. = teaspoon
lb. = pound
Evoo = Extra-virgin olive oil

Oven Temperatures

300 F = 150 C
320 F = 160 C
340 F = 170 C
360 F = 180 C
380 F = 190 C
400 F = 200 C
480 F = 250 C

Conversions

1 ounce = 28.34 grams
1 pound = .453 kilograms
1 g = .035 oz
1 kg = 2.2 lb.
1 fluid oz. = 29.57 milliliters

Measuring Spoons

1 Tablespoon = .5 fluid oz. or 14.79 ml
3 tsp. = 1 Tablespoon
4 Tablespoons = 1/4 cup
16 Tablespoons = 1 cup

Notes

CPSIA information can be obtained
at www.ICGtesting.com
Printed in the USA
BVHW020954211221
624584BV00015B/1070